The First Time Home Buyer Book

Michael J. Wolf, GRI

First published by Dog Ear Publishing
4010 W. 86th Street, Ste H
Indianapolis, IN 46268
www.dogearpublishing.net

ISBN: 978-160844-575-2

This book is printed on acid-free paper.

Printed in the United States of America

ACKNOWLEDGMENTS

I WANT TO THANK my wonderful wife Jessica and my wonderful family. Their love and support have made my life accomplishments possible. I want to thank my editors, Chiwah and Matt. Their help with the editing process brought this book to life. I also want to thank my two mentors, Penny and Ken, for their help and guidance, their professionalism, and their utter dominance of the real estate trade to help me get where I am today. I also want to thank those clients who encouraged me to make this book. They told me they looked for a book like this and couldn't find one written since the 1970s. Lastly, I want to thank you for purchasing this book. It was easy to write, because it came from the heart. I hope you enjoy it, and that it helps as a phenomenal resource guide for the purchase of your first home.

INTRODUCTION

T<small>HE PURPOSE OF</small> this book is to make the largest purchase of your life as simple as possible. Buying a home today is like break-dancing in a minefield – one wrong move, and the whole thing can blow up in your face! After reading this book, you will be able to grace your way into your first home without the risk of everything going to pieces.

In all seriousness, the word "challenging" comes to mind for a first-time homebuyer in today's market. From the search, to the financing, to the numerous hurdles and pitfalls, the foreclosures and short sales, the buyer-seller dynamics, what your friends are telling you to do, what your agent is saying, what your significant other is telling you, and so on, it's tough to navigate your way safely into your new home.

Coming from the standpoint of a Professional Realtor that works everyday with first time homebuyers, this book provides an accurate and realistic account to give you the best perspective as you embark down the path of homeownership. This is not a dummy-book or an idiot's guide! This book is filled with real world accounts of great examples of what to do and what not to do so when it comes to your first place, so you can learn from my collective experience and benefit as a result. This book will guide you through each and every step of the homebuying process, from the minute you decide on buying a home all the way to the close of escrow. The process is part of the adventure! This is the largest purchase of your life, but a good education will reduce your stress level and make the process fun and exciting.

When I first got into real estate, I was also in the market to buy my first home with my brother. I figured I would use myself as a guinea pig for my first real estate transaction; if I messed up, I would only be hurting myself. This was a long time ago, and back then all I needed to get a loan was to fog a mirror and tell the lender how much money I needed! Obviously, things have changed since then, but I remember how much of a whirlwind the home buying process was. My parents were involved to some degree in the home selection process, but when it came down to the nitty-gritty details, my brother and I didn't really get the guidance we needed; we just jumped in and hoped for the best. I didn't know whether I was making the best decisions, and after finding the home we eventually bought, it was difficult to comprehend all the documents that were thrown at us. I didn't know how to interpret everything and separate what was important from what was not important. As I was my own real estate agent, I had no one but myself to lean on.

We still own that house, and since then my team and I have helped countless others buy their first homes. From my own experience and the experiences of my many clients, I have collected a wealth of knowledge to make you a savvy homebuyer. This book will arm you with knowledge of what to do, what to expect and what questions to ask when buying your first home. Simply put, my goal is to make you look less like a first-time novice, and more like a seasoned veteran real estate buyer.

When I think about the main issues that come up with most of the first-time buyers I am helping today, it comes down to a few simple (*simple*, not *easy*) issues. Most of these have to do with failures to manage communication and emotions. These two factors are of utmost importance, but how can you be expected to know what to do when you haven't bought a home before? After reading this book, you will have gained an understanding of what works and what doesn't, what to do and what not to do. This book will help you find out how to go about making your first home purchase a positive and rewarding experience. This process is only as stressful as you allow it to be! With the right mindset (realistic, reasonable, and positive) and the necessary information and help, you are sure to have success with your big purchase *the first time!*

I can help only so many people on a face-to-face and case-by-case basis. This book is the fulfillment of a longtime desire of mine to have the ability to help far more people than I can help in a given year of real estate sales. I have always wanted to write a book, and by writing a book about buying your first home I can be the trusted advisor and real estate consultant you need to help you through this process. Your friends and your parents mean well, I'm sure, but they probably don't know anything relevant to your situation today. Unless they are professional real estate investors, or involved directly in a related field on a regular basis, what they think they know or what they might have heard may not apply to today's market or your particular situation.

Most first-time buyers find it hard to trust a real estate agent, and instead rely on much less accurate information supplied by parents, friends, relatives, and the media. Sad to say, this forms a bad foundation for a homebuyer's education; it is my hope that this book can create a strong and accurate base of understanding for your first home purchase. Furthermore, this book underscores the importance of finding a good agent who will be able to advise you well and turn your expectations and goals to reality. Having a great realtor makes it much easier to navigate the current market and not look like a deer in headlights throughout your transaction. You need not go it alone. What you do need is a solid professional to help you along the way.

BONUS: Among others, a bonus feature of this book is free access to a referral database of real estate professionals from around the entire country who can provide you with the level of service that I provide my San Diego area clients every day. If I cannot help you directly, and you have nobody to turn to for a solid Realtor referral, I am here to help. Good thing you bought this book!

You should use this book as a resource throughout your transaction; it is designed to help make the entire home-buying process easier. I also want you to share your success story, so at the end of your adventure, please do log on to my website at www.thefirsttimehome buyerbook.com and let us know how it went. Be sure to send pictures of the wonderful home you bought!

Also, you will be given several "bonus" items throughout the book. These extras will help you with your home buying process and add depth to your homebuyer education. Happy reading, and happy house hunting!

This book will follow the process of buying a home from beginning to end, chronologically. I will include common questions, definitions, and pitfalls in each section. If you experience an issue that isn't specifically addressed in this book, you are welcome to e-mail me to let me know what you are going through. If your problem, issue, or story is sensational enough, I may include it in the next edition.

The most interesting thing about what I do is that no two clients or situations are ever the same. Every transaction is completely unique. As a result, there are thousands of potential hurdles, pitfalls, problems, or errors that could lead to costly mistakes or even the unraveling of the transaction altogether. Because of this, the book will be presented in such a way as to offer you the most comprehensive and easy-to-follow way to go about your first purchase. If you really want to get yourself into a new house, read the book in its entirety, then consult each chapter and make notes as you progress through the home buying process. It will keep you focused and ensure that your home purchase goes smoothly.

One time a fellow named Al came into my office. We had met at an open house and had agreed to an appointment to discuss getting him into his first home. As it turns out, Al hadn't done his homework: his credit report had more derogatory claims and collections reported than he had actual trade lines. (This is really bad.) It was apparent that Al was in no position to buy a toaster, let alone his first home. Being prepared is the only way to start down the path to home ownership without the bumpy ride. Al was the type of guy who leapt before he looked. Since you have purchased this book, you are already NOT like Al. Way to go, but we aren't done just yet.

So You Want to Buy a Home?

There are many reasons why people decide to buy a new home, but whatever the reason may be, preparation is all-important. This book is not about *why* you should buy a home; it is about *how* you should buy a home. I'm assuming you have already committed yourself to this all-important purchase. No matter what, my only advice is that you be certain you want nothing more than to buy a home. This way, you won't waste everyone's time! When the pressure builds, and when problems creep up, rather than running for the hills you will have the confidence to move forward. Because you have made this decision, you *will* become a homeowner!

PART 1

CHAPTER 1
FINDING
THE BEST LENDER

HAVING A GREAT lender on your side makes you entire experience so much easier. Your most important people in your real estate transaction are your agent and your loan broker. Make sure that both of them are AWESOME!

If I came to the realization today that it was time for me to buy a home, the first thing I would do is find a lender I could trust. Any time I talk with new clients or referrals, one of the first couple of questions I ask is whether they have been prequalified or preapproved by a lender.

There's a difference between prequalification and preapproval. These terms get thrown around a lot, and they are not the same. Between the two, preapproval is better. Prequalification is like telling a loan officer about your financial situation over the phone to see whether things jive with what you are trying to accomplish. Preapproval is a full-blown credit check with verification of your assets and income. Because people always embellish their personal situation, a prequalification may not be accurate or offer much insight. It's like asking a lender, "If I make about this much, and I have this credit score, and I am looking to get a loan for so many dollars, do you think I can get the loan?" This is kind of ridiculous: there's no reason for the lender not to say "Of course!" just to get you in the office! For these reasons and more, preapproval is the way to go; the numbers never lie when they look at your financials and check your credit, and when you are preapproved by a trustworthy lender, you can be confident that you will be able to get a loan.

The best lenders are the ones that you are referred to. TV commercials and lenders you find on the web are NOT COOL. These are shady lenders that may sell your information to other sources, or "get" you with a teaser rate that's only available for perfect borrowers with spotless credit, who make way more money than you. On the other hand, your brother's friend's uncle that does loans part-time from his home office doesn't fit the optimal description of a good loan officer either. It all comes down to who you know, or who you can get connected with.

When looking for a good loan officer, there are a couple sources to consider. You could ask your Realtor for referrals. In fact, a professional agent that works with lenders every day is the BEST person to ask for a referral to a lender. We Realtors know which lenders do their job the best, and which to avoid. If one of your friends or family members just closed a transaction and had a positive experience with a lender or loan officer, this would also be a terrific place to start.

BONUS: At the end of this chapter, I will list the most important questions you will want to ask when you meet with a potential loan officer.

BANKS VS. BROKERS

There are two very different kinds of loan officers: *mortgage bankers* and *mortgage brokers*. Put simply, a mortgage banker works at a bank that offers loans, while a mortgage broker finds a loan from one of several banks. There are benefits to each, and neither way is clearly better than the other: it all comes down to personal preference.

To go with a mortgage banker, walk into the bank and say to the banker, "Hey Mr. Banker, I would like to apply for a home loan!" The banker will sit you down, and offer whatever loans that particular bank is offering at that particular time. The Banker might say, "Do you want Loan A, Loan B or Loan C?" By contrast, a brokerage has dozens and dozens of relationships with banks, putting a lot of options at its disposal. After all, every borrower is different, and every bank offers different guidelines for lending. If you are self-employed, certain banks might not offer you a good loan. Similarly, maybe you are a teacher or government worker or in the military; some mortgage brokers specialize in these professions and would do a much better job than a typical big bank loan. A good mortgage broker will be able to find a solution (a good loan that fits) for most borrower types. Other issues that would cause a borrower to need to look elsewhere than the largest banks are if you have a smaller than average down payment, less than stellar credit, or the need for a larger allowance for closing costs, or if you are financing a condo that has issues with the HOA, among many, many others. The list of things that lenders scrutinize changes weekly. This really emphasizes the point that, no matter whether you use a bank or a broker, the person you actually deal with must KNOW HIS OR HER STUFF INSIDE AND OUT. Research, ask questions, test them, and pick the best person. May the best and most experienced loan person win your business!

Is there a difference in costs between a mortgage bank and mortgage broker? Yes. For the most part, using a mortgage broker tends to be a bit more expensive in terms of the closing costs for your loan. Why? When you go with a brokerage as opposed to a big bank, your loan officer has a greater need to make a good impression and establish a relationship with you. He (or she) wants to do a job deserving of any referrals you may send over after a successful transaction. Your loan officer can be contacted directly, and you will establish a personal rapport and business relationship together. He will hold your hand the entire way throughout the transaction. Contrast this with a bigger bank, where you will still have a loan officer, but where the personal touch can sometimes erode. Of course, there are wonderful loan officers at the larger banks, but you should expect to get a bit more "hand holding" when you work with a broker. This being the case, they typically get compensated more for dealing with you on a more frequent basis.

Sometimes the big banks offer deals and incentives a broker just can't match. In order to get more loans closed, a big bank can give better deals, perhaps waiving the closing costs or offering rates that are not profitable to a smaller mortgage broker. Be savvy, ask a lot of questions, and do your homework. I love to talk, and I love it when my clients call me with questions about these types of things.

Banks and brokers both have loan officers working for them. Your job is to make sure you get the warm and fuzzy feeling with your loan officer when you meet initially, and at the same time stay clearheaded and focused. Your loan officer can literally make you or break you, so make the right decision as to who will get your business.

There's one more factor, and you can take this one to the bank (pun intended). Sometimes it's not the best rate, but the best *fit* that you should be looking for. Some lenders just listen and take your order, without offering any alternatives. For example, some people go into the bank dead-set on a 30-year mortgage even if they're just planning on being in the home for four or five years, as if 30-year fixed rate mortgages were the ONLY way to finance a property. This is certainly not the case. As I write this book, 30-year rates are hovering around 5%, but the 5/1 Adjustable Rate Mortgages are in the 3.75% range! This can be a lot of savings for a loan that is a better *fit* for the borrower. Ask questions, and be a savvy borrower. At the end of the day, you have a lot of people who are there to help, but you are responsible for making sure you get a beneficial outcome.

I had one client who categorically refused to use a mortgage broker. He swore it would cost too much. He went into a big national bank and spoke to someone who seemed to be the "loan guy" at the bank. It turns out the fellow he talked to was some banking specialist, not a loan professional in any way. When the time came for my client to "lock in" his loan rate, I asked the banking specialist what the rates were for that day, and *he said he did not know*. When you trust your business to a bank, you expect to work with someone who at least knows something so rudimentary as the going mortgage rate for the day. Worse, this poor fellow's file was sent all over the country in the bank's computer system, from Florida to Los Angeles, at various points in the process. About a dozen people touched his file, and he had very little ability to call and ask questions of any one person familiar with his file. This was frustrating and stressful, and it could have been avoided had my client made sure to work with a loan officer or mortgage professional from start to finish. So no matter where you go or who you work with, make sure that the one person who will be handling your file from beginning to end is a genuine loan officer. This way you have one person to call the entire time.

Bonus: What Is an Adjustable Rate Mortgage?

When you see "5/1 ARM" in reference to a loan, this means that the loan is fixed at an initial interest rate for five years; then, one time each year after that, it readjusts to a benchmark index rate (usually the US Treasury or the LIBOR rate), plus perhaps a margin of profit for the lender, always spelled out clearly in the paperwork. A 10/2 ARM is fixed for ten years and adjusts two times each year thereafter.

My father took out a 5/1 ARM loan on his second home, fixed at 5.2%. After five years, it adjusted to an index where the rate was (then) 1.25%. The lender had a 2.25% margin, so the benchmark (adjusted) rate of

1.25% plus the margin of 2.25% gives us his new mortgage rate, a lovely 3.5%. Adjustable rate mortgages aren't always so bad! When rates go down, they can make a good rate even better. Check out the resource guide at the back of the book for more on this and for current rates on the most typical loan types.

Shopping Around

Do all your shopping for your loan before you spend any time looking for homes. Don't waste precious time in escrow trying to figure out who will give you the best rate and terms; you should have this all figured out before you look at your first house. This is because when your offer on a home gets accepted, you have a concise timeline to make sure you get approved for a loan. If you run past your deadline and find out that you can't qualify, *you may lose your initial deposit for the property.*

What's more, your loan officer will need one hundred percent of your focus and attention, and as much time as possible, to build your file, get the necessary financial information and application paperwork, and submit to the underwriter (the god of the lending world) for approval. If you are speaking to multiple loan officers under this timeline (called the **contingency period**, or due diligence period), you may not be able to get the approval on time. Worse, as I said, you can lose your deposit if things go sour.

Also, loan officers may not want to deal with you if you are still shopping around during your contingency period. After all, they know you are setting yourself up for potential disaster, not to mention affirming your lack of faith in the process. Avoid this situation. Do the shopping around at the beginning, and choose a loan and loan officer that fit your needs *before* you go any farther.

The best start to the process might be to find three good mortgage referrals. I usually give my clients three or four business cards from the loan officers I use most. I give referrals to both mortgage brokers and banks so my clients have options. When you shop around, do ask each loan officer for a **Good Faith Estimate** (GFE), which should be provided free of cost. This allows you to compare lenders on an apples-to-apples basis. A note of caution: a lot of charges (closing costs) need to be estimated in the GFE, so they make an educated guess on these fees. An example of this is escrow and title charges, which are not specific lender charges. Some lenders estimate high or low with these costs, and some lenders don't estimate at all, which would bring down their total cost to make your loan. Just be aware of what they are estimating and compare it to the others. Don't hesitate to ask your Realtor about any questions pertaining to this. A good Realtor can help with most general questions about this process for your loan.

> **BONUS:** Check out the resource guide in the back of the book to see what your typical Good Faith Estimate (GFE) looks like.

CLOSING COSTS

Closing costs are all of the costs paid by the buyer for the home purchase over and above the purchase price. A lot of ancillary services go into a home purchase; most people just don't realize this until the transaction has closed. There are loan, escrow, title, courier, notary, insurance, appraisal, credit check, and several other fees that accumulate throughout the transaction. The lender's portion of the total closing cost amount is almost always the biggest chunk.

Closing costs tend to range from about $4,000 to $9,000 depending on the purchase price and circumstance and they could be higher. This means if you are putting down 20% on that $300,000 house (that's $60,000, for the mathematically impaired), the total you need to come up with at the close of escrow is the $60,000, *plus the closing costs*. For this reason, a lot of buyers opt to include a closing cost credit in their offer to offset the additional amount of monies needed at the close of escrow. More on this later.

At the end of every transaction, the escrow company handling your transaction will send you what is known as a **HUD-1 Settlement Statement**. This will show you where all the money went, and will specify all the final closing costs.

> **BONUS:** I have included a sample HUD as part of the resource guide at the end of the book so you can see all the different charges a typical buyer can expect in a given transaction. I will address closing costs in chapter 4, but for now, it's enough to know that they exist and what they are for.

Be Prepared. Get Preapproved.

When I am dealing with a client who has already spoken to a lender, I know the client already has an idea of the home price or monthly payment desired. This takes a lot of guesswork out of the equation, and puts the buyer way ahead of the game in terms of preparation and focus. Furthermore, many buyers find mistakes on their credit reports during this process. Getting preapproved before beginning the home search will give you the time to address any problems and fix your report so your credit score goes higher. When clients come into my office for the first time with the preapproval in hand, and they know what they are looking for in a home, it eases the process for everyone involved. Simply put, being prepared goes a long way. Taking the time to get the right information together will make everything easier in the end.

THE WRONG WAY: GETTING A LOAN AFTER FINDING THE HOUSE

Let's take an opposite approach – what's the worst that can happen? Let's say you come into my office, ask to see some homes, and refuse to get preapproved. Usually I would just turn you away, but for example's sake, let's say I take you on. We go and look for homes, and you find the perfect place after months of searching. We make an offer, it gets accepted, and we open escrow.

Now you have a very tight timeframe to make sure this is the home for you and get approved for a loan. You have 17 days to determine that this house is all good or cancel the deal, and you don't have a clue which lender or loan program you'll end up with. You don't know exactly what your down payment is, and you aren't sure of your credit. Against my advice to call the lenders I have recommended, you decide to go through lendingtree.com because they are offering a 4% fixed rate loan. After several days, you find out that you are not qualified for their program and end up going with my lender.

Now, seven days into the escrow, you are getting documentation to the lender and are finally making headway. By day 10, the lender gives you a "conditional thumbs-up," but you are wary and still think you can get a better interest rate. You are considering calling in on the Ditech 800 number because they are offing a fantastic rate as well, but you aren't telling me or the lender about this. My recommended lender pulls your credit and finds that your credit score is 607; without some repair, you won't be able to get a loan. The worst part is that your score is so low because of a correctable error that just needs time. This stinks; there is no way to do everything we need to do to get you approved for the loan in time!

In this scenario, you would be forced to back out of the agreement; otherwise, the seller would get the drift and cancel at the first opportunity! This is what happens when you do not go in prepared. Even if your credit were good, you would still be in a bad position were your loan not approved during the contingency period for any of a million reasons. You should not look at homes without being fully vetted for the loan you need. No good agent would show you any homes until you show them that you are approved, and thus worth their time.

So, if you are hot and heavy about finding a new home, then go get preapproved.

> **BONUS:** For some great referrals to lenders in your area, check out the resource guide in the back of the book to email our team. We can give fantastic referrals for nearly every part of the country – even Alaska!

Typically, any lender will need the following minimum documentation when you are meeting up to get preapproved. Collect this data and contact us if you need a good referral for a lender to get started.

- Your driver's license;
- Your most recent two years' tax returns and/or W-2s;
- Your most recent two months' bank statements (all pages, all accounts);
- Your most recent two months' statements for all asset (stock, 401K, IRA, etc) accounts;
- Your most recent two months' pay stubs;
- Authorization to pull your credit.

GETTING YOUR CREDIT SCORE HIGHER

There are a lot of myths concerning credit reports and what goes into determining your score. Google "**FICO**" if you don't believe me. Everybody has heard something from someone, and most of the time the info is false. So be skeptical, and do your homework. That said, here are a few pointers on maintaining and possibly improving your score before you get preapproved. For some, nothing short of professional credit repair will be able to improve their credit score.

Bonus: if you are one of these people that need professional credit repair assistance, check out the resource guide at the back of the book. We will be happy to refer a professional to get you in the right direction, and this starts by getting your credit in good shape. This typically takes a few months to accomplish so get on it now! The sooner, the better.

When it comes to boosting your score, consider the following steps:

- Keep credit card balances below 30% of the total credit limit. This will help boost your score, especially if you are consistent about it. This goes for all of your credit cards. If you are unable to pay the balance down below 30%, try calling your credit card company and get a credit limit increase so that your balance is proportionally lower, relative to the limit.
- Do not make any large consumer expenditures on credit before a home purchase. This sounds obvious, but you would be surprised how many people buy a car, a luxury, or a big appliance on credit, pushing up their debt and reducing their ability to borrow prior to buying their home. (PS: Buy the stainless steel appliances *after* you close escrow!)
- Maintain credit lines, even ones with zero balances. If you really want to cancel a card, it's not going to make *that* big of a deal (I did for a department store card that I opened to save on one large purchase), but for the most part keep your credit lines open.
- Don't be late. Late payments kill your credit, especially those that are past due for 60 and 90+ days. Pay your bills on time all the time. You will not get a loan with more than 1 late payment within the past year! Get in line, pay on time, and

call the professional credit repair referral found in the resource guide in the back of the book if you need help fast.

- If you see a discrepancy on your report that you think you can fix yourself, go to the big three credit bureaus' websites (Transunion, Equifax, and Experian) and look for the links to reporting an error on your credit report. Depending on the circumstance, they are usually pretty good at addressing errors within a few weeks. For anything more serious, a professional credit repair company is generally worth the cost.

MYTHS ABOUT CREDIT AND YOUR CREDIT SCORE

This helpful information is borrowed via mint.com and from Experian.com. Credit is due to them to help address some of the most common urban myths about your credit score and credit reporting.

Myth 1: Checking your credit will lower your score.

Checking your credit report will never affect your score. Thanks to the Fair Credit Reporting Act, you're entitled to one copy of your credit report a year from each of the three major credit bureaus. You can order them as many times as you want (by paying for subsequent reports) and it still won't adversely affect your score. If you do apply for credit by filling out an application, though, your score might be slightly pinged.

Myth 2: Shopping around for a loan will hurt your credit score.

Not anymore. In 1999, the scoring model was changed so that consumers wouldn't be penalized for comparing rates within a 30-day window, says Heather Wagenhals, author of the Unlock Your Wealth crisis management and financial wellness series. However, if you shop for a credit card one day, a boat loan the next, and a mortgage the day after that, the underwriter may wonder whether you were denied or if the loan hasn't hit your report yet.

Myth 3: If you don't use your credit card account, you'll lose your credit line.

As a credit fraud measure, your lender may stop reporting your trade line for lack of activity, says Wagenhals. "Your scoring is based in part by open and active trade lines," she says. "Thirty percent of your score is based on timely payments. If there is no payment due, you may be missing out on a possible one-third of your credit score." According to Wagenhals, it's much better to charge your credit cards up to the amount you can comfortably pay off each month and rotate cards to keep them all open and active.

Myth 4: If you co-sign on a loan, your credit score is not affected.

According to Patrick Ritchie, author of The Credit Road Map, when you co-sign on a loan, you are equally liable (along with the primary borrower) to repay it. This debt will appear on your credit report and will have the same ramifications as if it were your debt exclusively. "Consider the payment ramifications," says Ritchie. "If you have co-signed for someone and he or she is 30 days late on the payment, it will hurt both of your credit scores. In the case of co-signing on credit card, they may pay on time, but if the card is maxed out, the impact on both credit scores can be dramatic."

Myth 5: It's impossible (and takes forever) to dispute information on my credit file.

By law, the credit bureaus have only 30 days to complete an investigation on your credit file – all you have to do is request it, says Gregory B. Meyer, community relations manager at Meriwest Credit Union in San Jose, California. "If they cannot determine the validity or accuracy of an item or if it was determined to be out-of-date/expired, it is supposed to be removed from your credit report," he says. When you mail your investigation request to the credit bureau, Meyer adds, you must mail copies of the request to the creditor as well.

Myth 6: After saying "I do," your credit scores are married, too.

It's a common misconception that credit scores are united in marriage, says Ken Lin, CEO of Credit Karma, a credit-score management service based in San Francisco. While you may share financial obligations in marriage, your credit scores will remain separate.

However, your spouse's credit habits can affect your credit score, specifically activities like paying bills on time. "If your spouse has had credit problems in the past, make sure he or she is committed to a healthy credit future before you agree to co-signing or opening a joint credit account."

Myth 7: Turning to a credit-counseling service will hurt your score.

"Credit counseling by itself most definitely does not hurt your credit score," says Ken Clark, certified financial planner and author of The Complete Idiot's Guide to Getting Out of Debt. "There is no place to report such a thing on the actual credit report, which is the basis for your credit score."

According to Clark, this myth surfaces because of people who end up working with for-profit debt settlement agencies that deceptively market themselves as "credit counseling." When these organizations negotiate a repayment plan or debt settlement on your behalf, says Clark, this can cause a drop in your credit score, since it is a further demonstration that you were unable to handle your use of debt wisely.

BONUS: QUESTIONS TO ASK A LENDER

When interviewing a lender, these are some of the must-ask questions. Make sure the lender understands that you are trying to find the most competitive rate, but that you are also looking for the professional that can provide the best service, advice, and fit for the loan program of choice.

- "Can you provide a good-faith estimate?"
- "Do you work with first-time homebuyers a lot?"
- "How long have you been in this field?" (A minimum of two years is a must!)
- If you're addressing a mortgage broker, "How many banks do you work with or have access to?" Anything close to 30 is fairly decent, and over 50 is super.
- If you're talking to a banker, ask "Why should I choose a large direct lender over a mortgage broker?" Also, "Do you have any special promotions or incentives for home loans right now?"

CHAPTER 2
FINDING
THE BEST REALTOR

REAL ESTATE AGENTS don't get enough credit for the work they put into their clients. There is a lot of potential liability in the real estate career, and true success takes sustained hard work. Many try, and few survive. A good Realtor should become your trusted advisor. By understanding and appreciating what the Realtor does for you as the client, you can guarantee a wonderful working relationship with your Realtor and ensure total success throughout your home buying process.

Always, when I say "real estate agent" I want you to think *Realtor*, and to consider only a *Realtor* to represent you in your home purchase. "Realtor" is a professional designation for a real estate agent who has made a public commitment to a high level of accountability and professionalism. A real estate agent merely signs a license; a Realtor adheres to a code of ethics.

With a Realtor, you can expect someone who has invested time, money, and energy into the real estate profession, as opposed to someone who paid a couple hundred dollars, took some classes and passed a test. Yes, a license allows one to practice in real estate in the state of issuance, but it says nothing of the agent's reputation. Most first-time homebuyers don't even know to ask, "*Are you a Realtor?*" or even better, to check out the agent's business card to verify their title. A Realtor can also take additional education to gain special designations, further proof of effort towards professionalism and competence. Usually, the more designations the better: few would spend the time and money on these designations without a passion for this business and the clients they serve.

Finding the right Realtor is hardly an exact science, but a little research can go a long way. In so many cases, the best agents are not the ones you see and hear about; on the contrary, the best agents are the ones who are so good at their trade and profession they don't *need* to spend money on advertising. These are the agents who work primarily by referral or word of mouth and have qualified people coming to them every day. This phenomenon only happens to great agents who know their trade and have built their business over enough years for new clients to seek *them* out.

Referrals Rule

Many buyers start by looking at agents they have heard of. This could be the local Century 21 branch next to the coffee shop down the street, or it could be that nice old lady who walks down the block every Thursday with her funky flyers. That old lady agent is desperately hoping that her hard work pays off and that after years of delivering her funky flyer to you, one day you will pick up the phone and call her. Similarly, the local Century 21 branch is hoping that next time you get coffee, you will walk in and become their next lead (and potential client). After all, they pay good money for the visibility that has been building their brand awareness every time you passed by and saw their sign over the years.

These are some of the many examples of how agents try to get your business, but you should not concern yourself with them. You should actively *seek out* a Realtor. Essentially, the best agents are typically the ones who don't need to spend time cold-calling or door-knocking to get their business. Business comes to them via referrals from past clients who are satisfied with their professionalism, honesty, and results. Take the initiative and give yourself the best opportunity to win: choose your agent carefully.

Let's take a moment to clarify this issue about star agents and how they go about their business. Great agents did not get that way by sitting around waiting for business to come to them. Rather, their success is the result of years of hard work building their businesses and spheres of influence in order to get to the position where they no longer need heavy marketing. Please don't mistake an agent's aggressiveness for a bad thing. A proactive agent is a very good sign! He or she is just trying to see where you are in terms of the buying process. An agent needs to know whether you are looking to move next month, or are looking to start looking next month – there is a huge difference! Sometimes agents who don't need to advertise do so anyway in order to maintain an identity in the community. Just as choosing the best agent is not an exact science, neither is the way that great agents market and advertise themselves.

Knowing what I know, if I wanted to find the best real estate agent for my first-time purchase, I would follow two basic plans: I would ask several people I knew and trusted for Realtor recommendations, and I would scan the online community consumer blogs for highly recommended Realtors.

BONUS: Alternatively, of course, I could go to my own website and submit my info, and we would find me a wonderful Realtor referral in my area. We have a strong network for Realtors and can help you get what you are looking for. Check out the resource guide in the back of the book to get you started.

As I mentioned before, the best agents are the ones who get consistent referrals. You should be one of those referrals! You should ask everybody you trust about his or her most recent experience in real estate. Preferably, you want to ask people for potential referrals who bought their homes recently, though a referral to an agent someone has worked with multiple times is a great sign. Always keep an open disposition for what people are telling you. In general, we humans have an innate need to share good experiences, so you should take any recommendations with open arms and then qualify them with questions about the experience. Whenever I get a referral from a past client or good friend, I am excited! I am already going to have a more solid connection to the referral, and there is a good chance the new client and I will mesh in terms of personality.

I will ALWAYS treat clients referred to me by people I know at a higher level than online "leads" or other unknowns. Without question, the level of commitment on the part of the buyer is so much more significant when it's a referral from a good source. I don't like admitting that my initial treatment of an Internet lead compared to a referral is different, but in practice it most certainly is! I can depend on a referral; I cannot depend on an online lead. For this reason I give priority to my referrals, and reserve the best service for them. Ask around, get referrals, check out the agents' websites, pick out your favorites, and schedule a time to meet.

Before you meet a potential agent, write down your most pressing questions. This will really help with your interview. It may be necessary to let the agent know you are interviewing a few other agents. This will keep them on their best behavior and you will see the best that they can offer. Usually I dislike it when I am referred a client who is "shopping" other agents, but here's the bottom line: If I were in your position, I would want to shop around until I meet the realtor who is going to represent me in the most important buying decision in my entire life. It is a good idea to shop around, even if it hurts the agent's feelings. The one you choose will probably forgive you.

In some cases, you may feel so strongly about a particular agent that you don't find it necessary to interview other agents. There is nothing wrong with this, so long as you feel very certain about it. It's typical to see that with a highly referred agent only one appointment is needed to see that they truly are the best fit for you. You'll probably be sold on them after that initial consultation. After all, there is a reason they are that good in the first place.

THE WOW AGENT

You should test-drive your potential agent during the interview. You're hiring your agent primarily for their real estate expertise. Their most important assets are their local knowledge (of the market, prices and inventory), their ability to negotiate and handle contractual issues, their ability to manage emotions and surprises, and their ability to connect with you as a person and help usher you at your pace through the transaction. How do you know your Realtor's skills before you begin? Ask questions! Your agent should leave you saying "WOW!" and feeling excited about the process ahead. Keep an eye out for that "WOW" agent. You will know when you find him or her, and you will be happy you did!

I cannot tell you how many times people have come to me looking for help after they have been working with a non-"WOW" agent. Sometimes the agent's problem is a lack of knowledge, sometimes it's a lack of communication, sometimes it's an unforgivable mistake, but no matter what, if you have found yourself with an agent you thought was a "WOW" agent, and you turned out to be wrong, it's OK to move on. My only suggestion is that as soon as you realize that your agent is not a "WOW" agent, you must cut ties with that agent as soon as possible! I say this because a lot of people are generally so afraid of confrontation that they negatively affect themselves in the process by not severing the relationship with the non-"WOW" agent.

Do yourself a favor. Be bold. This will help you get what you want quicker, and it will be a wake-up call of sorts to the agent.

The bottom line is simple: go with a pro. Go with someone who knows the trade, and who is aggressive and tenacious (in a good way). Go with someone who knows how to talk and negotiate. Go with someone who has it together. Go with someone you connect with on a personal level – this will help you to build trust with your agent, and trust is the most important aspect of the agent-client relationship. Once trust and respect are established, the rest will fall into place. Just make sure you have the agent who will get you what you want.

> **Bonus:** As a gift for purchasers of this book, we are offering you an amazing resource to help find the right agent. This Realtor database consists of fabulous agents across the country who work like I work, and it will be invaluable if you don't have any great referrals to go off of. Just call us or check out our website to let us know where you are looking to buy, and we will hook you up with a great agent immediately and completely free of charge.

It is important to remember that no matter how you choose your agent, being a good client will pay off in the end. Being demanding or demeaning to your agent will get you nowhere. Go in with the intention of keeping your agent as a trusted advisor for anything real estate-related from that point on. A long-term relationship is better for both parties, and no agent will tolerate an extremely needy or demanding or rude client for long!

When I work with clients who have this kind of commitment to the client/agent relationship, there is no end to what I would do for them to ensure that their experience is second to none.

Bonus: The Top 10 Characteristics of a Great Realtor:
It's important to know what differentiates a so-so Realtor and a WOW Realtor. I believe that these are the most important characteristics to look for when determining

the professional that is going to assist you with your purchase.

1. Experience: At least 2 years is a must! Nothing compares to experience when it comes do knowing the real estate trade. Experience teaches you what problems to avoid, allows one to know what is typical and atypical in a transaction, and makes the deal smoother in so many ways.

2. Expertise (in the location and property type you're dealing with): A person who specializes in the downtown region won't know the inventory or the values as well as the Realtor that specializes in the suburbs. Also, if your Realtor really specializes in commercial real estate, but is helping you with your residential transaction, that lack of specific residential knowledge can come at your detriment.

3. 1st impression could end up being the last impression: What is the first impression you get from your potential Realtor? If you're not "Wowed" move on. You should feel inspired and excited with your Realtor, so if it is anything but, do consider someone else.

4. Professionalism: It's OK to get along with your realtor but he's not necessarily there to be your friend, he's there to advise you and work proficiently with you and the other agent. You want to make sure that your Realtor exhibits all aspects of professionalism. Look for use of vocabulary, dress and etiquette, and how they respond to difficult questions.

5. Speed of communication: If your calls/emails aren't being answered in 24 hours or less move on. This

says a lot about how hard your agent is willing to work for you.

6. People Person: Your agent should be on the ball and connecting with you and everyone else that is involved in your transaction. She should be polite, sincere, not too pushy, and someone that gives you the sense of urgency when you need to make an important decision.

7. Negotiation and contract skills: Your agent should know contracts inside and out; when they are explaining the contract to you they should sound confident and proficient. It's a bad sign if the agent is reading the contract with you during the appointment. Further, you should get a good sense of the ability of your agent to negotiate on your behalf. When it comes down to crunch time, you want to make sure that she doesn't buckle under pressure; you want to be ensured that your agent will truly go to bat for you.

8. Integrity and Honesty: A Realtor ascribes to a higher code of ethics than your typical real estate agent. They are your fiduciary, meaning that they should be acting in your best interests at all times. If you have the slightest hint or suspicion that your agent is anything but, it's time to look for a new one.

9. Designations: These entail a further dedication for one's profession. (The more, the better). For example, I am a GRI (Graduate of the Realtor Institute). I've spent time and money furthering my education and awareness of my industry, career, expertise, and experience as a result.

10. Going above & beyond: An agent that consistently goes beyond the call of duty to exceed your expectations is one that you can fully confide in and consider as your trusted advisor well into the future.

Bonus: The Top Ten Traits of a Successful Client
A recent client of mine named Amanda embodies this mentality. Her purchase price was low, which meant I wouldn't get much of a commission. The job entailed many hours of work, several offers, a long short-sale escrow and a couple of delays. All this was of no concern to me because of the type of client Amanda was. The time and effort involved didn't matter, because she was top-notch. I wish all my clients were like her. In fact, I have said during the course of transactions with several clients that I wished all my clients were like the one at hand. Whenever I say this, I am saying that this particular client exhibits the following qualities, and no matter the challenge at hand, I am there without question to make sure everything goes right.

1. Be reasonable! Don't get too emotional, ever. When clients get overly emotional, agents get impatient. This is a grown-up world and you need to act like an adult. I will hold your hand throughout the transaction, but irrational clients never get the best treatment.

2. Be responsive! Unanswered phone calls and ignored emails are never a good sign. This is a warning flag for an agent, signaling that you may not be as motivated as you say you are.

3. Be punctual! If I am on time, you must be on time, too. This is a simple thing, but it's surprising how many people are late to everything. This is a slap in

the face and you lose points in my book if you are late to confirmed appointments. If you flake on an appointment, start looking for some other agent; I probably won't work with you any further after a stunt like that.

4. Be flexible! Sometimes your wants don't quite line up with your budget, and you need to be OK with that! An irrational client is the last thing I want, a big waste of time. Really, it means that the client doesn't know what they truly want, or that what is affordable for them (what the buyer can actually buy) will not work.

5. Be honest and upfront! The more honest and open you are, the better I can serve you. Sometimes I go weeks with a client, only to find out about a preference, financial condition, or special need that has not been addressed. This can seriously affect the client's ability to find something that will work. Open yourself to your agent, and your agent will be better equipped to find you what you are looking for!

6. Be grateful! Show some love for your Realtor. Show that you appreciate all the time and hard work put in for your benefit. A grateful client is easier to work with and gets more appreciation than a demanding client.

7. Be respectful! This is a business, and you are dealing with a professional. Treat your agent like you would want to be treated yourself. When I am treated without respect, I have no problem moving on, letting go of a potential client. Sometimes clients seem to feel a need to act condescending or big or strong to establish control over the situation. This behavior is not

conducive to a mutually healthy and beneficial business relationship.

8. Be trustworthy! I want to trust you and you should want to trust me. When both the client and the agent have a relationship built on trust, nothing can stop them. It's only when I have clients who question me as to my skill or ability that the relationship becomes distant.

9. Be prepared! Be ready to move fast! I know you are a busy person, but buying a home takes focus and commitment. I don't care if you had a busy week; we have a lot of documents to go over in a short time, and I shouldn't have to feel bad asking you to go over things you should be going over through the course of the escrow. I am bringing to your attention items and issues that will directly affect your purchase and the home you end up with. I cannot want the home more than you do, and if you aren't prepared and committed, it makes everything more difficult and stressful for me and for you.

10. BE COMMITTED! Being committed means that your heart and mind are in harmony with respect to the goal at hand. I have found that this is the number-one trait for all the buyers in my most successful and seamless transactions. When a buyer is committed, no matter the hurdle that may arise in escrow, the buyer will overcome. When the buyer is committed, the entire process is less stressful. When the buyer is committed, success is in the cards.

Bonus: Google Your Agent!

Today's online community offers an exceptional ability for any consumer to check in on the history of their service provider's reputation and work ethic: kudzu.com, yelp.com, and angieslist.com are a few stellar examples of websites geared to service providers for a specific geographic location. As time goes on, more and more of us will become connected, and this type of virtual "feedback" will become more and more pervasive.

Real estate aside, you can and should be doing this for any service provider, from your babysitter to your auto mechanic. That said, at least a nominal amount of online research should be called for to find any specific warning flags regarding the agent(s) you are considering working with. Check the agent's website and see if there are written testimonials on the site, and if these testimonials match up with what you find online. Keep in mind that there are some people who just love to file complaints, even for good service, and this can tarnish your expectations of the person you are considering working with. Please know that the online community cannot be fully regulated for accuracy, but it is typically more helpful and accurate as opposed to being burdensome and untruthful. There is no doubt that this kind of research will become more common because it is user-generated and tends to offer a comparatively unbiased opinion of a given service provider.

Choosing the right agent won't necessarily make or break your deal, but it can mean the difference between a satisfying deal and an unfulfilling one, a good deal and a not-so-good deal, a one-time transaction and a trusted advisor for life. Put simply, choosing the best agent gives you the best opportunity to realize massive success for your first home purchase. Choose wisely!

CHAPTER 3
FINDING YOUR HOME

Now THAT YOU are preapproved and have chosen your Realtor, it is time to find that home. If you are unsure of exactly what you are looking for, you may need to take an hour or so with your agent to get acquainted with the areas you may consider and the current market trends, and also to isolate what exactly you are looking for.

The search is the most exciting part of the process for a first-time homebuyer. Have fun, take notes, take some pictures, be reasonable, and be efficient and responsive with your agent.

Sometimes people come into my office with a specific vision of what they want. They know what is reasonable, and it's relatively easy to find them a home. Other clients may need a tour of the areas that support their budget. I consult with most new clients for an hour or so, asking questions about the particular new home they have in mind, what it looks like, what it needs, how it needs to work for them and their daily lives, what they hate about their current habitat, and so on. All this will help provide me with a foundation for looking for homes based on their defined criteria.

It is important to know what you are looking for *before* your agent starts sending you properties from the Multiple Listing Service (MLS). If your agent knows what you are looking for, you can save time and effort by only looking at homes that fit your needs and budget. Some work at the beginning really helps improve the quality of the results.

Once I meet with the client and get a good idea of what will work, I do a search and send them the results. If no further tweaking is needed, the client reviews the results and chooses their favorites, and we go see their favorite choices in person.

The way I do showings and searches may not necessarily be the way your agent does them. Every agent has his or her own philosophy, and there is no true right way to go about it. It just comes down to making sure you are comfortable about the process. For example, I see on HGTV shows where the agent just picks out a few homes and the buyer settles on one of them. I understand how some buyers may come into my office expecting me to do all the work – researching, choosing, and showing you the property – but I have found that nobody knows more about what you want than you! The more you are involved in the process, the better the results. If my client is selecting places to see, there is no bias on my part. I do the search and filter out the duds, and my client picks the best ones. I find that this is the most efficient way to go about it.

Some of my clients go further in this process and actively search on their own on a daily basis. When they find a house they want to see, they contact me. This is wonderful: it's less work for me, and we only spend time looking at places they have selected. Either way, your agent will cater their service to your style and preferences.

WHERE DO MLS LISTINGS COME FROM?

In most markets today, there are several "types" of sales. You have heard of a few of them, but I want to take a moment to address the most common types of property sales you will come across in most markets across America.

Equity Sale: In an equity sale, the seller has equity in the property, meaning the property value is more than any amount the seller owes on the home, or the home is owned free and clear. This is the most seamless and buyer-friendly transaction. In some areas, equity sales are rare due to distress sale inventory, but in normal markets, these kinds of home sales are the most common.

FSBO: FSBOs are For Sale by Owner – This is an owner trying to sell the home on his or her own. You can usually find FSBOs in the newspaper or online, but not on the MLS because they aren't working with an agent that would put it on the MLS. In a FSBO, you can assume that the owner is either too cheap to hire a professional real estate broker or thinks that he/she can do a better job than the real estate professional can. This can leave the door open for potential litigation and extra liability on the part of the seller. Real estate is generally not the seller's trade, so you cannot expect the seller to act like a professional. The seller may miss details and not be on the ball by comparison to a real estate professional.

Regardless of the price a FSBO home seller is asking, have your agent calculate the savings from that FSBO seller not paying a commission to a listing agent, and make your offer with that savings in mind. Most FSBO sellers find that buyers offer them a price that is low enough to negate any perceived savings, and the seller has done all that work for nothing. They usually don't "get" this until it has already happened, so just do it! Many smart buyers won't consider FSBOs unless the market just doesn't have what they are looking for. Ask your Realtor about this type of sale as more of a last resort.

Foreclosure Sale: Foreclosures (properties sold by a bank or corporate institution) are pervasive in most markets today. A foreclosure happens when the lender takes a property back from a buyer who has stopped making payments on the loan. (By the way, the terms "foreclosure", "REO" (Real Estate Owned), "Repossession," and "Bank-Owned" all mean the same thing.) With a foreclosure, you are dealing with a giant institution, and you *will* play by their rules and jump through their hoops if you want the home. (I will touch more on this in chapter 6.) Foreclosures aren't always super deals; they are just another type of property listing that has different quirks compared to other property listing types. In all cases, the financial institution turns the property over to a local listing agent. This agent reports to the asset manager at the institution, and their relationship progresses with each property. It is in the listing agent's best interest to get the financial institution the best offer possible, as this enhances his or her prospects for acquiring more listings from that institution. It's always good to follow the money.

Short Sale: A short sale occurs when an owner owes more to the bank than the property is worth, and asks the bank to accept the loss in order to sell the property to a new buyer. A few years ago, most banks didn't have a short sale department. However, in a downturn this type of thing does happen, as declines are seen in both home values and people's ability to pay their mortgages. Those who bought in the recent years of historic high prices are facing a real issue in today's depressed market. Borrowers who lose their income are less able to pay on their mortgages, and may request that the bank accept a loss on account of their circumstances.

Short sales are fairly complicated transactions. The seller is still involved, and must approve any offer on the property. In addition, the seller's lender must also approve all aspects of the transaction. There are essentially two acceptances required, one from the seller first and then the bank. The biggest complaint about short sales these days is about how long they take. The reason for this is that most banks are absolutely inundated with short sale offers and do not have the staff to handle the workload in a proactive, efficient manner. Still, some of the best deals I have ever negotiated have been short sales. The reason is the incentives inherent in the deal. In a foreclosure, the listing agent works directly with the bank to get the highest price possible. In a short sale, the listing agent isn't necessarily looking for the highest price, but for a patient buyer who understands that short sales take a while. After all, each time a buyer gets sick of waiting and drops out, the listing agent has to start the short sale process all over again. Sometimes the buyer will be offered a better deal to create the incentive to stick around for short sale approval. When I am listing a short sale, I want to find a preapproved buyer who understands the dynamics of a short sale, and make sure the buyer knows that this one offer is the only one being considered by the short sale bank; all others would be considered as backups. The buyer puts an initial deposit down to affirm that he or she is emotionally and financially invested in the deal. (Note: If the listing agent does short sales in a way that does not give you, the buyer, an exclusive, fair chance of getting a short sale acceptance, then you should walk on the property.) Out of all types of home sales, a short sale is the most complicated and the most time and labor-intensive. That said, you can get a steal if you are patient and aggressive about getting a good offer accepted by the short sale bank.

Miscellaneous: Almost all homes available on the market for first-time homebuyers will fall into one of the categories above. That said, you may run into government-seized properties, "probate" properties sold as a result of the owner's death where the court may be involved in the sales process, affordable income housing, age-restricted communities, or other quirky property or sales types. A good Realtor will be able to see and explain the differences between all available properties, as well as the consequences and benefits of any opportunities available.

TIME TABLES

Typically, an equity sale lasts as long (in escrow) as the buyer and seller agree. If they agree to 14 days in escrow, then that's what it is. If the parties agree to a 60-day escrow, so be it.

In a foreclosure, escrow is typically 30 days. Expect no nonsense from the bank, and if you take longer than the agreed upon time you may end up paying money each day until closing (This is known as a "per diem" fee).

In a short sale, if the seller accepts your offer to be submitted to the bank, the short sale approval process can take up to six months, but usually takes 90 to 120 days. What determines this length of time are several variables that are beyond the scope of this book. Once the approval by the lender is acquired, the escrow process can begin and you can then make steps to close the transaction. The actual escrow period is usually 30-45 days. All in all, it can be a long wait, but it is usually worth the time invested.

WHAT TO LOOK FOR IN A HOME

Whenever I tour a home, I always try to get the best feel possible emotionally for a place while at the same time trying to judge the property in terms of condition, quality, and other tangibles. MANY times you only get one shot and less than a single TV show's worth of time to accurately judge the worth of a home and store everything in your memory bank. It is important to take as many quick notes as possible, and even pictures to help jog your memory. This process can be challenging, so let's take a moment to consider what factors you should consider when looking at a home.

Curb appeal: No matter what, if you wouldn't even consider the home based on the location or what it looks like from the curb, then *pass*. You don't need to humor your agent. Move on to your next prospect right away.

First Impression: When you first walk in, get a read of your first impression and emotion upon entering the space. If you get a generally negative or generally positive feeling, take note.

Checklist: Every buyer (and if you are a couple, do make sure to work together) should make a checklist of the *most* important traits or characteristics of a new home. Write down your MUST-HAVES for your new home. This list should not be exhaustive; rather, it should comprise a few "non-negotiables" for the house you are going to buy: a walk-in closet, an open floor plan, a large master bedroom, a fireplace in the living room, whatever. Sometimes your Realtor can help filter for these, but some attributes, like walk-in closets, are not "searchable" on the MLS. This checklist is of critical importance. It should consist of five or fewer items.

Condition: Lean into your Realtor a bit for this. Realtors are hardly building inspectors, but they have seen enough homes to know how to identify some potential repair items. You will get a more detailed look at the condition when the inspection takes place, once your offer is accepted and the home is in escrow. Nevertheless, take into account whatever you see that may need to be addressed.

Upgrades: A lot of times, significant upgrades are almost necessary to make a home decent. One that comes to mind is the dreadful popcorn ceiling. Although you can live with it, you would rather live without it, so you may want to ask your Realtor for a good drywall referral. The same goes for other important fix-ups that are not immediately necessary but that you will want to do in the near future. This should factor in on your decision of what to offer, and your Realtor can help with this.

Even if you like popcorn ceilings, you should think as if you were going to sell the property in the future. What are the turnoffs? If you were going to sell the home in a couple of years, what would turn most buyers off? This should factor into how you value the property. Sometimes it can be small bedrooms, a busy street or an airport flight path, an aging condo, a really high HOA fee, a small galley kitchen… it could be anything, and everyone has their own opinion, but do your best to come up with a list of problems. With a little luck, this list will be shorter than the list of positives!

Ask a neighbor. Sometimes the best info on a house, neighborhood, or condo complex comes from the neighbors. They will spill the beans and let you know everything you could possibly want to know – they are sometimes even *too* helpful. I make a point to do this every time, especially if my client is looking in a condo complex. I will ask a neighbor about the complex itself, whether there have been any issues with the HOA or litigation, or whether anyone may be experiencing construction problems or defects. I ask about the complex's or neighborhood's attitudes toward pets, and about the general feel of the complex itself – what's it like to someone who lives there? These are all things you should find out now. You don't want to move in and then learn that your next-door neighbor likes to play rock music until 2:30 in the morning on weeknights. This is the kind of problem that can generally be avoided by asking the right questions and letting the neighbors talk.

If after all this analysis you are still bullish on the home, you should make an offer right away, especially in a hot market. You don't want to lose the place because you stalled; if you like it and it fits, move on it. This is even true if it's the first home you've seen! Sometimes I just show the right house first, and my client hesitates to write an offer because he hasn't seen enough places. Don't be that person. Write the offer – it's a good learning experience at a minimum — and see what happens. If it wasn't meant to be, then go see the other stuff. Sometimes the first house you see is the best one, especially if your Realtor knows what you like.

That said, don't rush yourself. Take notes and pictures to help you make an informed decision on any home you are considering. Many times, I have had buyers who fell in love with a home, made an offer, and got accepted. Then, during the inspection period, they started to notice all the dirt and dust, the hairline cracks, all the little inadequacies and faults of the home. Finding a house that fits all your criteria is a fun and emotional process, but a little condition analysis will mitigate any surprises that may come during the inspection. Remember to ask questions of your Realtor. Although your Realtor may not know all the answers, a good one will know how to get the answers, or at least point you in the right direction. There is a learning curve to the home searching process, but with a positive mindset and a good agent on your side, you can find the home you have been looking for that much faster!

How Many Houses Should You See?

This question doesn't come up much, but it is important. When you go out to look for property, it's important not to see too many properties in one sitting. I have found that my clients don't like to look at more than eight homes per day: ten is the absolute maximum. Looking at more homes *feels* productive, but after you see ten places in one day they all begin to mix together in your mind. Keep in mind that few Realtors will object to showing you more than eight or ten properties in a day; you will have to manage this yourself. What I try to do when I am showing a property is identify its most obvious feature. If a house has a pink mailbox, it's the "pink mailbox" house; similarly, I showed a place where the owner had a dog in a cage, and it became known as the "sad dog" house. This makes it easier for my client and me to discuss a property; it's easier to remember than "the house on 33rd Street," or comparing the place on Swift to the one on Robinson. Finally, when you are looking at property, keep in mind the home you like most and compare each successive property on all criteria to the current "favorite" that of the moment. This will eliminate the duds.

CHAPTER 4
MAKING AN OFFER

SOME PEOPLE GET discouraged if they don't get the first house they make an offer on, and may even quit the process altogether! There are always other fish in the sea, as the saying goes, so don't let an initial failure get you down. Use it as a learning experience, a lesson that will help you with the next place. Staying positive, excited and optimistic is a surefire way to assure that you will find a home you'll love.

After you've found a property that hits on all of your predefined criteria, or when you walk into the place and you know it could be the one, talk to your agent about making an offer on that home.

IT'S OK TO MAKE OFFERS

When the time comes, you should place an offer on the property right away. I have had several clients who were hesitant to make that first offer. I can understand a certain level of anxiety about getting to the point of taking the initiative and sign a contract, but you are trying to buy a home, right? So when you find a home that meets all of your criteria, or one you can seriously see yourself living in, *make that offer!* Maybe it's a commitment thing, but all of my clients who were hesitant at first have felt relieved after the singing of the contract. In hot markets with a lot of competition between buyers, you will find yourself making a lot of offers, because many of them will get beat out by other buyers.

I once had a client who offered $90,000 above the list price to remain competitive because about twenty other offers had been placed on the property. Although she lost out to an all-cash offer, she eventually was given a chance to get the property (and we did negotiate for better terms) because the all-cash buyer backed out. When it comes to the offer process, anything can happen, so stay positive no matter what!

You must look forward to writing that offer. This should be an exciting moment rather than an anxious one. Also, don't become frustrated if your offers don't get accepted. As long as you are making reasonable offers, one of them will be accepted. It is important to stay active, positive, and responsive to the process, and to work with your Realtor to help make your offer better and more presentable so that it stands out against any other offers on the property. More on this later.

Let's talk more about the strategy of making the offer, and then about presenting the offer.

STRATEGIZING YOUR OFFER

Coming up with the offer that will work best for you depends on three main factors:

1. The local market (up/down, hot/cold, buyer's vs. seller's market)
2. Comps for the property (to establish or justify the offer you are making)

45

3. Competition for the subject property (multiple offer situation)

Let's address each of these separately:

The local market: A cold market, one in which nobody is writing offers, is considered a "buyer's market." In such a market, there is little to no competition for most homes on the market, and inventory tends to be higher than normal (more than a six-month supply of homes on the market). Buyers can negotiate most terms in their favor, as the market is characterized by sluggish activity, languishing sales, and declining prices. Given the state of the market, no sane seller will want to lose you as a buyer, so they will do their best to work with you and will typically make concessions (in price and terms) in your favor. Conversely, in a hot market prices are typically on the rise, and many buyers are out looking at a (typically) limited supply of homes. A lack of supply and an abundance of buyers means sellers hold the leverage in negotiations, and such a market is known as a "seller's market." This market is characterized by rapid sales, rising prices, and multiple offer situations. Whether you find yourself making an offer in a buyer's or a seller's market will affect the way you and your agent create the offer.

Comps for the property: The "comps" determine the value of a home in your general market. A typical comp is a home that has sold within the past three to six months and is similar in location, size, and relative condition to the property you are considering buying. If the home you are looking to buy is listed for $300,000 and the comps are hovering around $250,000, that constitutes justification for offering a lower price. Be mindful of the comps, as this is how the seller and listing agent should have come to the selling price in the first place. A realistic seller will list a property near or at the price point of the comps. Furthermore, banks sometimes bring a property onto the market at a severely reduced price in order to attract several offers. Most of the time, the multiple-offer scenario and bidding-war environment lead people to go higher than they would otherwise go, and the price that wins the house is higher than it would have been had the property been brought onto the market at the going price of the comps.

Often, a seller and/or listing agent will fall back on the comps if you try to write a low-ball offer. You will hear, "You offered *what? Haven't you done the comps?!?*" Nevertheless, in a market with no competition for the property, making an offer lower than what the comps suggest would be acceptable, though your agent may hesitate for fear of creating further downward pressure on the relative values in the area. Before you decide on making an offer, ask your Realtor for the comps to help you make a more informed decision. It's much better than going off of whatever gut feeling you or your Realtor may have.

A comp is a sold property. Sometimes a property is too unique to have many comps, so defining the value of a home becomes more of an art than a science. Comps are not "pending/in escrow" properties, and the other "active" listings on the market typically define the higher value limits in the local market. Work with your Realtor to get a good idea of the value of the property you're interested in.

Competition for the property (multiple offers): In the offering process, nothing complicates the buyer/seller dynamic more than a multiple offer situation. Such a situation arises when you write an offer and the listing agent tells you there are other offers on the table.

I once wrote an offer for a client on a home that ended up getting 73 offers. How ridiculous is that? The place came on the market at $170,000, ridiculously below the comps, and ended up selling at $340,000, slightly higher than the comps suggested. This was a bank-owned property, and they wanted to sell it fast for a good amount of money. This strategy paid off for them, but can you imagine trying to explain the situation to an interested buyer client? Sometimes things just get too crazy, and you may want to pass. Say "Next!" and go on to another property.

When it comes to a multiple offer situation, you have no way of knowing what the other buyers are offering. Because of this, you don't know whether they are undercutting the comps, going in at list price, or offering above list price. Depending on the market, you can make assumptions, but you never know for sure. That makes it difficult to figure out how much to offer.

I always ask (about other offers), but never tell. Do keep in mind that it is in the listing agent's best interest *not* to tell other agents what the offers are coming in at. *I always* make a point to ask, and sometimes they tell me. Why would I *never* tell? Out of consideration for my seller. What if the highest offer was $501,000 and the first buyer backed out? The next buyer might feel fine about offering several thousand dollars more for that property, but if the listing agent spills the beans by revealing the amount of the last offer accepted, then that buyer knows exactly what price to go in at!

When you have just one buyer and seller negotiating, things are fairly simple between the two parties. But when another offer comes into play, it changes the dynamic. Any good listing agent will play the buyers off each other in order to negotiate the best terms and price for the seller. Whoever wants the home more will agree to the seller's terms, and the house will be theirs, but only after conceding on potentially important terms and price.

Buyers usually don't overpay unless they fall in love with the property. Whatever you do, keep the comps in mind. Stick with your price and be prepared to maintain your position, even if it means you may lose out on the property. Every decision you make in the offer and negotiation process must be carefully calculated to minimize any potential regret. Your agent can help you out, but the final decision must always be yours!

Bonus: Navigating the Different Kinds of Markets

Specific advice for a down market:

- Be more aggressive. Most sellers will make a counter offer rather than cancel or reject your offer outright.
- Lowball offers are generally more acceptable – hey, you never know.

- Be prepared for longer negotiation periods.
- AWESOME TIP: Be ready to walk away from the negotiation table altogether. Sometimes this can be your best tactic. You'll smile when the listing agent calls your agent a week or two later to say they will accept your terms because nothing better has materialized.

Specific advice for a red-hot market:

- Be willing to make an offer at or above list price to beat other offers on the table. Lowball offers will be laughed at, and will not be responded to; don't waste your own and everyone else's time.
- Know that negotiations are typically very short, if there is any negotiation period at all.
- Expect terms to be in the seller's favor. To maximize your chances of getting your offer accepted, ask your agent to help you construct terms that will have more appeal for the seller.
- BE FAST! Take your best shot as soon as you know you like the place, rather than waiting for a counter offer that may never come.
- Have your agent call the listing agent and ask whether there are specific terms that might help your offer stand out above the competition, especially if all the offers are offering around the same price point. These may include issues like the length of time for the escrow, items that will not be included in the sale, specific items that won't be paid for, etc.

I will touch more on submitting your offer the best way possible later in the chapter.

CLOSING COST CREDITS

Closing costs are the costs ancillary to the transaction, over and above the price of the property. The cost to make your loan, the cost for the escrow company servicing the transaction, and all the other costs incurred throughout the process of the escrow are all considered "closing costs." Depending on the loan amount and the type of loan, they can add up to several thousand dollars. When you have spent several months, if not years, saving up a down payment for your home, the last thing you want to do is waste that money on something like closing costs. Most buyers don't even know what closing costs are, much less factor them into the equation of how much it's going to take to purchase a home.

Note that the loan and the costs surrounding the loan are always the lion's share of closing costs. For more on this, review chapter 1 again. Once you qualify for your loan, get the GFE (good faith estimate) to get a good understanding of how much the closing costs will be. Not only will the GFE show what the lender closing costs will be; they will also estimate the remaining closing costs for the escrow, title, etc. In most cases, closing costs average around $6000-9000. Keep this in mind, as it will affect your bottom line in the offering process!

With knowledge of how much closing costs can set you back, many first-time buyers make their offers with the seller paying for some (or all) of the buyer's closing costs. Take for example a property listed for $400,000 in a competitive hot market. I would offer $410,000 with $10,000 in closing costs, meaning that the seller would pay for up to $10,000 of my closing costs. To me, this means that if my total closing costs come to $11,000, I will need to bring in the additional $1,000 at the close of escrow. (If closing costs end up being less than $10,000, any excess goes back to the seller; if you don't use it, you lose it!) To the seller, it means that although the price is $410,000, the true "net" is $400,000, because $10,000 of the seller's proceeds is being credited to the buyer.

Make sure you get most or all of your closing costs covered! Sometimes the market doesn't really allow offers that ask for closing costs (this is sometimes the case for short sales), but as a general strategy, I always try to cover some amount of closing costs for my first-time homebuyers to lessen the amount needed to close escrow.

If you have more closing cost credit than you need, you can "buy down" your rate to help reduce the interest rate for your loan. To get a handle on this, envision a buyer throwing money at the loan up front to lower the rate. Talk to your lender to ensure that all of your closing cost credit is correctly allocated. (You can buy down the interest rate even if you don't have closing cost credits. You will want to have a conversation about this with your lender; keep in mind that there is a smart way to go about it.)

READ THE CONTRACT!

There are a lot of terms that will need to be explained in every contract, and you should go over the contract in full and get a thorough explanation of all terms. Without going into further detail, these are smaller items, but important to know nonetheless. I don't think it would be beneficial to go into this further here, but I suggest you take this next bit of advice seriously:

Be safe – READ THE CONTRACT!

Are you serious? I *know* that almost all of my clients haven't fully read the contract they are signing. Why would you do this for the most important purchase in your life up to this point?

I work in California, a highly litigious state. As a result, there is *a lot* of paperwork throughout the transaction, and about 16 pages on average for a typical offer. Although reading the contract for the offer can be construed as a common cure for insomnia, it is something you NEED TO READ. The offer is your road map to the transaction. It addresses anything and everything that could possibly happen or go wrong throughout the process of the transaction. In addition to taking your agent's word, you should review when you have more time to yourself after writing the offer. After you go through it once, you should be good to go for any successive offer thereafter. A buyer who is well versed in the contract (to the greatest extent possible) is a well informed buyer, one who is better prepared to face the problems, hurdles or pitfalls that can occur in the process of the transaction. Read the contract, write questions, and ask your agent for clarification to help you understand with what you are offering and agreeing to.

GETTING YOUR OFFER ACCEPTED THE FIRST TIME!

The way you present the offer can greatly affect your chances of acceptance. This is especially true when you are dealing with several offers on one property. Before fax machines, agents would make appointments to meet in person and discuss the offer. This exchange has been largely lost to the evolution of technology.

Today, you can easily go through several transactions without ever meeting the agent on the other side in person. If your agent takes it upon him/herself to present your offer in person on your behalf, it will truly make an impression upon the listing agent. These days, the closest thing to presenting the offer the way it used to be done is to send a cover letter or email with your offer attached, explaining the merits of your offer, your qualifications as a client, and a little bit about you. If presenting in person is too weird for you and/or your agent, consider preparing a cover letter representing you, the buyer. Talk about yourself, how much you love the home, and how you can see yourself living there and taking excellent care of the place. Pull on the seller's heartstrings, and include a color photo at the end of the page. This will make an impression on the seller's emotions. When there are ten offers on the table and the seller sees yours with a picture and letter expressing your love for their home, it may turn out to be the deciding factor.

One time my neighbor put her home on the market, but used a personal friend as the listing agent. I liked her home a lot, and had a client in mind for whom it would work perfectly. The home was very well priced and was totally charming, so it did get a lot of offers, but I had an ace in the hole. I knew the seller's favorite beverage! After presenting the offer to the listing agent, I self-delivered a six-pack, along with the offer and the buyer's letter and picture, to let her know I had submitted an offer on her home on my client's behalf. The entire gesture worked to our advantage, and all it took was a little creativity and a nine-dollar six-pack.

Get creative to differentiate yourself over the competition. Bake brownies, or offer incentives if you have a hook-up of some sort. Make the seller want to go with your offer. In some cases, with the right mix of creativity... even if your offer isn't the highest offer, you can compel the seller to go with you anyway. Now, that's what I call success! By no means am I condoning bribing the seller. I am just suggesting you get creative if the market is so competitive that none of your reasonable offers are getting accepted. When all else fails, innovate.

The moment you find out your offer has been accepted is the most exciting moment of your entire home buying experience – even more so than the close of escrow, in my opinion. The acceptance of the offer sets everything up, and the close of escrow is just something you wait for. The fun lies in finding "the" place – your new home. So... when this happens, celebrate it! And then get right back to focusing on the tasks at hand.

CHAPTER 5

ACCEPTANCE AND COUNTER OFFERS

So… you've gotten this far. You've made an offer on the property that works for you. Now what? Well, the seller can accept your offer or reject it, but more often than not your offer will get "counter offered" by the seller. We will address all three situations.

ACCEPTANCE

Sometimes an offer will get accepted as-is; the seller agrees to all the terms and signs (executes) the agreement. This doesn't usually happen, but it will if your offer is just that good, or if the market is such that there aren't that many buyers out there and the seller is happy to agree to (potentially all of) your terms. If you have a good agent, he or she will have spoken on your behalf with the listing agent before the offer was submitted to the other side, thereby garnering an opportunity to understand the behind-the-scenes dynamics prior to presenting your offer. This makes for easier negotiation and a higher probability of your offer being accepted right away.

It's a good idea for your agent to talk to the listing agent before you write the offer. This way, you aren't going in "blind." This fact-finding on the part of your agent will allow you to make a more informed decision about your offer. Have your agent ask specific questions about what the seller is looking for (if anything) in the offer. This could be anything from the seller not wanting to sell the appliances to wanting a 60-day escrow. Who knows? The point here is that your offer can become more appealing to the seller after your agent efficiently questions the listing agent. Some listing agents have loose lips and will tell you more than you should know. Asking specific questions is a good thing to do, especially when you're dealing with a multiple offer situation, as what you learn may have an effect on the terms you wish to present in your initial offer.

After an efficient conversation with the listing agent, your agent can convey information to you that can be used to entice the seller to accept your offer right away. This is especially imperative in a competitive market with many buyers vying for the same property.

REJECTION

It never feels good to be rejected. Most sellers will want to work with anything that comes on the table. You don't typically see an offer getting rejected, but if you are getting rejected and it is happening more than once, you may need to check to see if your offers are realistic. I'm guessing that you are making some serious low-ball offers that don't even get a counter offer. Check yourself before you wreck yourself.

COUNTER OFFER

By far, the most common response to any offer presented to a seller is a counter offer. The typical counter offer revolves around price, but many times there are "cleanup" items that are negotiated back and forth between counter offers. There are too many to list, but cleanup items can range from which title and escrow companies will be used for the transaction, to minor terms pertaining to timelines within the contract, to changing the initial deposit; it could be anything, but typically a counter offer will revolve around terms that will firm up the deal and make the seller feel more confident in the buyer.

A counter offer is basically the seller saying, "Hey, I like your offer; I approve of everything you have presented, with the following exceptions: 1) close of escrow to be 30 days, 2) price to be $480,000, 3) Initial deposit to be $10,000 4) escrow to be ABC Escrow Company 5) Title to be 1st Title USA." In response, the buyer can accept, reject, or counter the counter offer. If the buyer counters, this is known as counter offer #2, which would go something like: "1) Purchase Price to be $465,000." This goes to the seller, and again, they can accept, reject, or counter. This could go on and on....

My record for counter offers is eight. I am sure there have been more, but usually after five or six counter offers I prefer to rewrite the entire contract with all the terms included that were negotiated throughout the rounds of counter offers. This tends to make things cleaner, and a clean contract is less prone to "problems."

THE DREADED MULTIPLE COUNTER OFFER

A "multiple counter offer" situation is one in which multiple offers have been received on the property and the seller is making a counter offer to more than one buyer. The difference here is that when you get the counter offer from the seller, *and* you accept it immediately on their terms, it does not mean that there is an agreement, just yet. The seller can wait and see all responses to the counter offers that were sent out before coming to a decision on the best offer. The seller is clearly in the driver's seat in this scenario. The best way to deal with this potential situation is to make a super-strong offer in the first place that will compel the seller to take your offer without even considering making a multiple counter offer. Or, if you are presented with a multiple counter offer for a house you truly like or love, you can come back with a strong offer and/or terms that will compel the seller to take your offer over the others.

It has been said that you will feel some sort of remorse no matter how you handle a multiple counter offer situation. You are making a decision on price without knowing what the other offers are, and it can be a real guessing game. You have to go with your gut, taking into account your agent's advice and keeping the comps in mind. If you make a strong offer and it gets accepted, you may think *Darn, I paid too much,* and if your strong offer doesn't get accepted, then you think *Darn, I didn't offer enough!* The bottom line is, if you like the property, go for it! If you don't get this concept the first time around, after a couple times of losing out, you will grow to accept this logic, I promise! You shouldn't be afraid to be bold on the offer, assuming it makes sense logically and financially and the house really "does it" for you. Go get that house!

WHAT NEXT?

So… they accept your offer! The process isn't complete until you are made aware of the seller's acceptance of your offer, and then either you or your agent must "confirm" your acceptance. Your agent can explain this further when you get to this part of the process. For all intents and purposes, when the seller accepts, you convey your confirmation of their acceptance, and then you have what's called a "fully executed offer." Now you are able to open escrow and begin the escrow process.

Note that you cannot open escrow until escrow receives a contract signed by both the buyer and seller. Also, you cannot fully get your loan underway until there is a fully executed contract; work on the majority aspects of your loan cannot begin without it.

PART 2

CHAPTER 6
ESCROW

From my experience, escrow can be the most misunderstood aspect of the transaction; buyers just don't understand what goes on behind the scenes. If you want to make an impression on the escrow officer handling your file, make a point to go meet her/him/them with some chocolate and a "thank you" for helping you realize your goal. It is important to build some rapport with escrow; if there is any sort of hitch in the process, an escrow officer willing to go the extra mile is handy indeed!

Opening escrow is exciting! It is a small but incredibly important step in the process of getting to your first home. Before I go any further, I'm going to talk about the concept of escrow in general.

WHAT IS ESCROW?

I remember when I first started working in real estate and hearing about this mystical "escrow" thing. I think it's funny now, but I didn't have a clue as to what escrow was, what it did, or how it worked. You may be as much in the dark as I was.

Really, there are two related terms to cover. If a property is *in escrow*, the property has an accepted offer already, but the sale has not been completed. At the same time, *escrow* is a company that acts as an unbiased, third-party intermediary between the buyer and seller during the escrow process. Escrow is the neutral go-between that helps to facilitate the transaction based on the contract.

Why Do We Need Escrow?

Why do we need a neutral third party? Can you imagine doing a real estate deal with just the seller? Think about all the ways it could go wrong! Escrow lubricates the deal to make things fair and easy. They hold funds, order reports, set up the funding of the loan, and deal with the county recorder, and provide a number of other services. Sometimes it seems like magic, but you would be surprised to learn how much the people at escrow do to make the transaction work. They are truly the unsung heroes of the transaction.

Escrow can never act unilaterally. They need mutual instructions from the buyer and seller in order to do *anything* other than what was specifically approved in the contract. Some escrows are better than others, and which escrow company is used or which side picks the escrow company should be spelled out in the purchase contract. Ask your agent about this, and make sure the chosen escrow company has a good track record.

Ideally, you the buyer can name the escrow company to oversee the transaction. In many hot markets, where the seller has leverage, the seller will get to pick the "services" of escrow and title.

Bonus: The best way to write the contract in that case is to let the seller name the escrow company that will help with the transaction, but *subject to the buyer's approval!* It would read "seller's choice w/ buyer's approval"

What can go wrong? A slow or inept escrow officer can cause problems you won't discover until crunch time. Make sure your agent stays on top of things by checking in with the escrow officer throughout the transaction to avoid surprises at the end.

ESCROW AND FORECLOSURES

Depending on the type of sale, the escrow process may not always be the same. Regular sales are one thing, but if you are buying a foreclosure (also known as a bank-owned property or REO), the bank will essentially *require* you to use the escrow company of their choosing. There does seem to be some conflict of interest here: how can an escrow chosen by the bank be an unbiased intermediary? The two are heavily intertwined; the escrow company gets a large volume of business from the bank, and doesn't want to lose the bank as a client. All you can do is hope for the best and pray that the escrow company isn't completely horrible.

Never forget this: dealing with a bank often means setting yourself up for unfair situations. This is just one of those many times you just have to "go with the flow" and jump through the hoops to get the property in question. Unless the market is very slow, the bank will tell you what to do and how to do it; if you want the house, you have no choice. I have found that the bank's escrow company is often slow to respond and not as on-top-of-it as you would want them to be, so your agent may have to really pester them to make sure they stay on the ball.

Another common issue with foreclosures is the time it takes to get important documents back from the bank. Getting a signature from some of the larger institutional banks can take a week or longer. The delays can get ridiculous, especially if you and your lender are working on a strict timeframe.

There is also the infamous **bank addendum**. In a typical foreclosure, your offer is accepted via a verbal acceptance conveyed by the listing agent out of the bunch of offers that were made on the property. The listing agent has either submitted all of the offers via email to an asset manager at the bank or talked about them over the phone. The asset manager makes the decision as to which offer to go with. At that point, an offer is *verbally* accepted, and the buyer will soon receive the bank addendum.

If you have made an offer on a foreclosure and your agent receives a bank addendum, this is usually a really good sign, because your offer was accepted (sometimes over several others). But after you go through the addendum, you start to see all the ways the bank takes control and tightens up the transaction. The bank addendum almost always tightens the terms and strips down your safety nets in the transaction, to make sure that you are a serious buyer and will do what it takes to close the deal as quickly as possible.

Moreover, the bank addendum completely supersedes the offer, so it should go without saying, just as with the contract, that it is of *utmost importance* that you read, review, and *understand* the addendum in its entirety. You need to know what you are signing, and also that the addendum is not typically subject to changes via counter offers. If you want the property, you must sign the addendum; it is as simple as that. If you don't like the addendum, don't buy bank-owned property.

Once you sign the addendum, the bank will send this and the contract to the bank's asset manager to sign off completely. Notice, now, that it can be several days after the bank addendum is signed by the buyer before it comes back as a fully executed offer. Note as well that, while the escrow timelines in a typical transaction begins when the contract has been fully executed, in a foreclosure the bank usually references the date on which they *verbally accepted the agreement!* This is tough to deal with, because while you are waiting around for the asset manager to sign the contract and get it back to you, your lender is unable to move forward without a fully executed contract.

The banks really don't make it easy for you. Not all banks are like this, but when dealing with a bank you must be prepared to deal with tough timelines and to acquire a thick skin to put up with what the transaction will require from you as the buyer. You will be thrown into a sea of paperwork. Do your best, and good luck! I wish it were different – It *should be* different, but most banks are too big and cold to care. They just want to sell the property as quickly as possible, and they're incentivized to make it hard for you to assure that you're serious.

On nearly every bank addendum, there will be a section referring to a per-diem fee to the buyer. This means that if you as the buyer cause a delay in the escrow closing, then each day after the expected close date you will be charged about $150. This is why it is so frustrating when the bank takes forever to get anything back to you. With this in mind, you should keep notes, and be sure to document every time the bank causes a lag in the escrow. If you are delayed in escrow, and if the delay can *in any way* be considered the bank's fault, have your agent get them to agree *in writing* to an extension without any per diem charge.

To recap, with a bank foreclosure, you only know you have a chance at the property when you get the bank addendum. Review the addendum carefully, because it is hard-core. Sign the addendum, and get as much accomplished as possible while waiting for signatures, because escrow is already open, the clock is already ticking, and you don't know how long it will take you to get your fully executed agreement.

Short Sales and Escrow

If you are buying a short sale, the contract will determine the course of the escrow. Each listing agent goes about short sales differently, and each bank has its own specific way of processing a short sale. This makes it difficult even to address short sales in this book. Escrow may be opened either before or after short sale approval. In the former case, once an offer is accepted it is sent to escrow, and the buyer waits for the short sale bank to approve the sale before making further progress. In the latter case, nothing happens while awaiting short sale approval. I will address each of these two methods, and why I believe one is better than the other, with specific examples.

In San Diego, there is one agent everyone strongly dislikes doing business with because of the way the agent does short sales. If I need to explain, I just have my client call the agent's main number to hear the agent's explanation of the short sale process, and all my clients say, "OK, no thanks!" Essentially, this agent puts a property on the market, takes the first offer received, and sends it to the bank without the seller accepting the offer. The agent then works with the bank to get the short sale approval. Meanwhile, other offers accumulate on the property. It may take four or five months for the bank to finally accept a short sale, at which time the agent goes back to all of the offers that have been placed on the property and asks for the highest offer among those still interested. This way, the agent keeps from opening escrow until the bank has approved the short sale and avoids having to work with just one offer.

In my opinion, this is the worst way to go about doing a short sale from a buyer's perspective. Why? Because you have no control over the outcome. You don't even know whether you have a *shot* at the property until several months after offering. Even after waiting for months, and after the bank approves the short sale, you look up and find yourself in a bidding war. It's the worst thing ever! Making an offer on a short sale like this is like hoping to hit the lottery. There is a better way!

The way we handle short sales, the seller signs and accepts one offer, and that is the only offer presented to the bank. All other offers are held as backup, to be used only if the accepted buyer backs out. This way, the buyer feels confident in his or her ability to purchase the property and is willing to stick around even if the short sale takes several months. This level of cooperation makes it easier to get the short sale approved and the deal closed.

In this scenario, the offer is accepted and escrow is opened during the wait for short sale approval. The buyer brings the initial deposit in to escrow, and in return, the property is put into pending/in escrow status on the MLS so that other potential buyers no longer see it as available. I have found that this way works best. The most successful short sale agents in the business go about their short sales in a very similar manner. This is why my team has a 100% success ratio with my short sales, and so many of the other agents' properties end up becoming foreclosures because the short sale didn't work out.

You should have your agent call the listing agent on a short sale to find out how they go about the process. Make sure the listing agent has actually *done* short sales before. Some agents employ specialized short sale negotiators for the short sale approval process. The specialist saves the agent countless hours on the phone negotiating with banks, thus shortening the approval process for all parties (in most cases). However, these negotiators come at a cost, and sometimes the seller or listing agent asks the buyer to pay for this service. Since everything between buyer and seller is negotiated up-front, work with your agent to assure the most beneficial terms for the short sale.

Keep in mind that everything is subject to short sale approval, and sometimes the banks refuse to pay for things that the seller typically pays for in a transaction. This means the buyer must come up with extra funds. Some of the most common items the bank might not pay for are the home warranty, certain closing costs, termite repairs, the seller's delinquent Home-Owners' Association (HOA) payments, transfer fees, recording fees, other small escrow fees, and just about anything else, on a case-by-case basis.

Keep your agent on the ball. Make sure the agent knows who pays for what, as this can increase your costs or even ruin the deal. Sometimes the only way to find out is to wait for the bank to respond to the short sale offer. They will review the file and say, "We approve, but here is what we will and will not pay for," and you either take it or leave it. Many times, the deal is a good one.

In its review process, the short sale bank will order an appraisal to determine whether or not your offer is acceptable. If your offer is too low in their opinion, they will require a higher purchase price. This makes it important not to deviate too much from market value on short sales. Sometimes the banks are just out-to-lunch and believe the property to be worth more than it is. Your agent may have to push for you, but often times the bank will eventually see the light if the comps justify your offer. In my experience most short sale banks have a minimum value requirement in order to approve a short sale. Depending on the bank, this minimum acceptable amount is 85-92% of market value. This is why short sales can be a very good deal – you just need to be patient.

Short sales are probably the most challenging of all deals, but some of the best deals I have ever put together for my buyers have been short sales. They are often worth the wait, if you just make sure that all agents involved have excellent short sale experience. There will be hurdles and bumps along the way, but hopefully this book can bring out the most common ones.

THE DETAILS IN ESCROW

Ever hear the saying "the Devil is in the details?" In real estate, it is so very true. Make sure your Realtor keeps moving, and you need to remain involved in the details of the transaction as well. So many times, clients get lazy or tired of reading important but tedious documentation, contracts, and reports. Because there is so much involved, it is common to see interest disintegrate and some documentation failing to get reviewed and approved. Do yourself a favor: stay focused on the details! You will thank yourself in the long run.

On receiving a fully executed purchase contract, an escrow company will open escrow and assign an escrow number. In a day or so, escrow will draft **escrow instructions**, stipulating the rules that govern the escrow process, and confirm the terms of the contract as well as the agents' commissions. The buyer will receive a set of escrow instructions to sign off.

Unless otherwise noted on the contract, your initial deposit is due within a few business days. Depending on how realtors do business in your area, it may be that the agent collects your deposit check when you write the offer, or that you are to deposit the check to escrow once the offer is accepted. I typically make it clear in the offer that the buyer will deliver the deposit check to escrow within three business days of the offer's acceptance. This is done when you write the purchase agreement with your agent, who should be able to advise you on this.

This is important: Your initial deposit is *not* your "down payment." The initial deposit is also known as your "good faith" or "earnest" money in the transaction. This deposit is the money you are putting into escrow to "hold" the property in your name until you either buy it or back out of the contract. If you default on the transaction, you can lose this deposit. Make sure when you sign your offer that your agent explains the specifics to your complete comprehension, as the rules vary from state to state.

CHAPTER 7

THE CONTINGENCY PERIOD

O K, SO YOUR initial deposit is in escrow and you have reviewed and signed your escrow instructions. What now? Now, you must make sure that the property you have under contract is truly right for you. You have a lot of work to do in the period before escrow closes, this is known as the **contingency period** (in some states it's called the **option period**). You also refer to this as the due diligence period.

What the heck does "contingency" mean, anyway?

A **contingency** is an event that occurs if a condition is met. In real estate, contingencies are conditions of the sale. When you are buying a property, your contract spells out all of the contingencies of the sale. Make sure your agent explains contingencies and the contingency period to your satisfaction.

Sometimes the buyer reduces the contingency timeline to make the offer look better. The typical contingency timeline on a California real estate contract is 17 days after acceptance. It is important to note that on foreclosures, most banks reduce the contingency period to 10 days on the bank addendum.

The most common contingencies are the approval of the buyer's loan, the buyer's ability to perform a diligent inspection, appraisal at or above market value, mandatory disclosures from the seller, "clouds" on the title report (see below), and, if applicable, the buyer's receipt of all HOA information. In fact, anything accepted by both the buyer and the seller can be made a contingency of the sale if agreed to under contract.

One time, a home I was showing to an interested buyer was right next to a freeway in the process of being expanded. Part of our offer included an addendum that made the freeway itself a contingency. More specifically, the buyer wanted to make sure the freeway wall was going to be high enough to suit him. That said, the contingency provided the buyer the opportunity to research the freeway wall height with CALTRANS to determine whether the height was satisfactory. This was a reasonable request, so the seller agreed to it in the offer, and thus it became a contingency to the sale.

One thing that's important to remember: if you cancel or back out of the contract after you have removed your contingencies, *the seller can take your initial deposit.*

During your contingency period, you must do whatever is required to make sure that this home you are buying is right for you. You will get your inspection, apply and get approval for your loan, and review all the reports and disclosures, addressing any issues that arise. Your contingency period is also known as your "due diligence" period, because you are doing your due diligence during this time to make sure that this property works on all levels. The seller expects you to remove all of your contingencies at the end of this period. If your contingency period is 17 days as stipulated in the contract, then by Day 17, you should have either removed all of your contingencies or backed out of the deal altogether. It is OK to back out of the deal without removing your contingencies; you will get your deposit back after canceling. However, if you remove your contingencies and *then* try to back out, the seller can claim damages and keep your initial deposit. This is why it is so important to work quickly and efficiently through your due diligence period.

Maybe the contingency period doesn't allow you enough time. If you need a few more days, you can sometimes get an agreement with the seller to extend the contingency period for an agreed-upon time. Also, the contract should have some provisions to keep the seller from withholding information from the buyer during the contingency period. If the seller delivers, say, a soils report to the buyer on the 17th day showing that the home sits on a major landslide area, and then demands that the buyer remove all contingencies, this is *not cool*. For this reason, the contract should allow for a mandatory extension of the contingency period when the buyer is delivered an important disclosure item.

This is one reason the contract is so important! It is the road map to your purchase, and addresses all aspects of the transaction in the event something goes wrong. *Review the contract fully*, and do your best to *understand this document!* With a better understanding of the rules to the game (the contract), you will be a savvier and better-educated buyer, better able to handle a hitch or impasse throughout the transaction.

It is important to remember that the nuances of the contract vary slightly from state to state. I am most familiar with California contracts; however, the logic behind the various U.S. states' contracts is similar, even as the wording and some particulars vary from place to place. I have purchased property in several states; after reviewing the various contracts, I've found they all say pretty much the same thing. However, this book may differ from your state's customs. Go with the flow, adapt to whatever variances you find, and above all, *read your contract!*

Now that you understand the importance of the contract and the contingency period, we can address some other important elements to consider with respect to the contingency period of the escrow.

Title Report: The title report addresses all items that pertain to a specific property's title. It is typically 15 to 25 pages long. If there are any back payments due on the taxes, any judgments or liens, or any weird stuff on the report that will hamper the property's ability to be transferred (known as **clouds** on the title), they will show up in this report. Depending on the issue at hand, the seller will want to handle any potential problem on the report prior to close of escrow. Only rarely is a title issue serious enough to ruin the transaction, but it does happen. If you are buying a condo, check the title report to verify the parking situation and any storage lockers deeded to the property. Also, the title report will disclose any specific restrictions on the property in terms of its use. Title reports are complex, so have your agent review it, too, and be sure to go over it together if it is too much for you. The title report is really an insurance policy on the title to your new home – it's your title insurance. Any issues that come up (not including the exclusions that the policy states upfront) will be taken care of via title insurance. However, title insurance payouts are really quite rare. Just be sure that the information that is provided in the title report (also known as the "PR" for Preliminary Title report) checks out and is accurate. You will typically receive the title report with the other documentation package that you get from escrow shortly after the escrow is opened.

Review of the Seller's Disclosures: By law, the seller must provide certain disclosures to the buyer. These function as a type of report card for the property by the seller, giving the seller an opportunity to let the buyer know everything they know, or have done, regarding the property. It is imperative that the seller discloses *everything*. If something were to go wrong down the line and it can be proven that the seller knew about the problem but did not disclose it, the seller can get into big trouble. In California, there are thirty-two different disclosure forms that are filled out in a complete transaction. That's a lot of information! Depending on your state, what is legally required and what is optional will vary. As a service to my clients, our purchase offer requires additional disclosure forms from the seller as part of our agreement, beyond the standard legal requirements. This extra info for the buyer helps in the discovery of important material facts during the due diligence period.

Disclosures are different in the case of a foreclosure as well as a trustee's sale, probate or estate sale. With these kinds of property sales, the bank/seller is often exempt from otherwise required disclosures. The main point here is that the seller has never resided on or used the property, so they know nothing about the property and make no warranties or representations; the sale is as-is. On the contrary, in a short sale, the seller is not exempt from these disclosure requirements, as the seller still owns the property and is responsible for providing this important information to the buyer. Essentially, disclosures help the buyer learn critical material facts about the property.

> **Bonus:** You should provide your inspector with a copy of the disclosures if possible so the inspector has an idea of what to focus on and pay extra attention to during the property inspection.

Property Inspection: This is one of the most important elements of your contingency period. The inspection is the first opportunity to pull the lid off of your new home and see what's inside. It should go without saying that the most important thing about the physical inspection is that you actually *do one!* I have had clients refuse to do an inspection, against my advice. Some clients are too cheap; others think they can do a good enough job themselves. Occasionally, I work with a client who has a background in construction. These clients may be the exception to the rule (even then I will urge caution), but for everyone else out there, and for *every* first-time homebuyer, I *strongly* advise that you not be a tightwad. Spend the couple of hundred dollars to get a trained set of eyes to give your new home a bill of health.

I have *never* had a transaction fall through because of the inspection. I'm knocking on wood as I type this, but when someone likes a home enough to buy it, any issues raised by the inspection can be overcome. I think this is a testament to my skill as an agent, matching the home with the client, and to the quality of my inspectors.

Bonus: Finding an Inspector. How do you find a good inspector? I have a few inspectors with whom I have developed a relationship of trust. I use their services faithfully, and with full confidence. Were I a first-time buyer, I would ask my agent for two or three referrals, call them, and have each one give me the references of their past three inspections. If you trust your agent, and your agent has a preferred inspector, go with your agent's choice. At the end of the day, a good inspector gets referrals, and a bad one doesn't stay in business.

Also, though inspectors aren't generally required to have licenses, most states have real estate inspector associations. In California, it's CREIA (www.creia.org). A glance at their first introductory paragraph says it all: *"A home inspection is an independent, unbiased review and report on a home's systems, components and conditions. Consumers and real estate professionals should expect no less than full professionalism, education, competence, credentials, knowledge, courtesy and an adherence to CREIA's Code of Ethics and Standards of Practice."*

Real estate inspector associations are a good place to find an inspector. Your agent's best inspector may be on vacation or otherwise unavailable. This type of organization can give you some assurance that the person you use to inspect your home is a credentialed professional.

I hope you don't need me to tell you this, but *you __must__ be present for your inspec*tion! This is something you cannot miss. You should schedule the inspection for as soon as possible once escrow is opened. For short sales, you can wait for the bank to approve the short sale to do the inspection, but why not do it earlier? If you find something that kills the deal, it is better not to have lost months waiting. The risk a buyer takes in this case is if the short sale doesn't get approved by the short sale bank (this happens from time to time.) Worse case scenario is that you will be out a few hundred dollars from the inspection.

While the inspector is doing the inspection, you should be walking your new home, taking notes and asking questions. Some of my clients shadow the inspector to see the inspector's findings in real time. Others don't want to intrude by peering over the inspector's shoulder the entire time. An experienced inspector has dealt with all kinds of buyers, so don't be shy. Do what feels natural. This is supposed to be a fun and exciting experience! Usually I schedule my agent's visual inspection, or AVI, for the day the physical inspection is performed. In most states, an agent is required to do a reasonably competent visual inspection of the property. I typically go over this inspection with my clients at the property. It's just a personal preference, one I've found quite efficient. I do my inspections and then the inspector goes over his/her findings separately, and by the end of it all my clients are advised by both of us and know everything they ever wanted to know about their new home.

Wear comfortable clothing to the inspection, and bring a snack. Depending on the size of the home and the thoroughness of the inspector, the inspection can last up to three hours. Also, you may want to bring your camera and a tape measure and take some pictures and measurements of the property to stimulate design and decoration ideas.

Beware of the Buzz-Kill! The inspector is being paid to do a *thorough* inspection, but some inspectors get a little *too* thorough in their reports, and over-kill the explanation of potential problems. This can result in freaked-out buyers, and overreactions are never a good thing. This sort of thing is a staple on HGTV, but because I have a solid inspector, I don't have to sweat it much personally. Of course, sometimes my inspector *does* identify issues that require attention from another service professional. If this happens, stay calm and get creative. Work with your agent on how best to address the situation. There is a standard procedure with how and when to request for repairs and your agent will explain if or when it is applicable to your situation as it does depend on the type of property you are buying. (More on this later)

Specialists: Think of your inspector as the general line of defense regarding knowledge of the condition of your property. If the inspector finds issues beyond the scope of his or her specialization, you will need to hire another inspector for the particular issue at hand. This costs money, but better to be safe than sorry. Some issue types that might require a specialist inspector are mold, plumbing, roofing, foundation, electrical, chimney, site/grading, and zoning/permits. This list could go on, but it's usually one or two of the issues named here that you will need, depending on the age and condition of your home.

Perhaps the property inspector tells you, "The roof looks pretty worn and is bowing inward in some places. This could cause drainage and leaking concerns, so I recommend that you get a licensed, bonded and insured roofer to come check this roof out." You would then have the roofer come out to give a professional opinion, plus an estimate for repairs. Finding the best service professional is a pretty similar process to finding the best inspector. Your agent is a great resource for this type of referral, because they deal with this all the time. I pride myself on having a terrific person for whatever the physical inspection calls for. To be prudent, especially in the case of a repair estimate, you may wish to get two or three opinions. Some of these estimates cost money and some are free. Do your best to keep costs minimal, but do expect to shell out several hundred dollars for these inspections. In retrospect, you will agree that it is a small price for peace of mind.

On average, between the month before and the month after the close of escrow, there are twenty-six services provided to the buyer during a real estate transaction. This is why you need to lean on your Realtor, and why your Realtor must have a good network of service professionals to call on. Twenty-six sounds like a lot, but when you count them up, you have the agent, the lender, the appraiser, the title company and title officer, the escrow and escrow officer, the notary, the inspector, the warranty provider, the termite inspector, and the HOA or property management personnel. Depending on the property, its condition, and your situation, you may also need movers, plumbers, roofers, electricians, foundation companies, site and survey engineers, and so on. This is why it is important to have an experienced and well-connected Realtor who already has solid relationships in place. Can you see how much easier such a Realtor can make this? Lean on your agent; help your Realtor help you!

So now you have your inspections done, and you have some issues of concern with the home. Using the roofing example mentioned above, let's say you had two roofers come out and both quoted about $5,000 worth of repair work to be done ASAP. What can you do about it? Well, it depends on the type of sale you have entered into, as well as the market. Your expectations with regard to repair requests or credits for repairs from the seller will depend on whether the sale is a regular one, a short sale or a foreclosure. On HGTV, sometimes you see the seller giving the buyer a repair credit for the cracked windows, or the aging water heater, or the dirty carpet, to make the sale go through. In our example, we have a potentially leaky roof that must be replaced. In a regular sale, the seller might give the buyer a credit for the roof work in a buyer's market, but probably not in a seller's market. If the market is hot, you may have to make room in your budget to fix the roof once you've bought the house.

In a short sale or foreclosure, you should expect to get no love from the bank in terms of the property condition, regardless of what the inspector says and any estimates and ensuing repair requests you provide to the bank/seller. When I am dealing with a foreclosure, I explain to my client that the banks will tell you time and again that the sale is "as-is" and that "seller will do no repairs." They say this upfront. The truth is, you can always ask, but you had better have a compelling request. By this, I mean the issue must be a health or safety item; cosmetic issues are rejected 99.9% of the time. Of course, if you are buying a fixer, then you can expect to get no repair credits, ever! You should make sure your offered price takes into account the condition of the home and the necessary repair costs involved. Similarly, in a short sale, the bank is even stingier with repair requests and repair credits. I almost never see them being approved by the bank. The reason for this is that when the banks accept a short sale, they are usually accepting a bottom-line "net" price that they must receive and not a penny less. This dollar figure takes into account all expenses they need to address and absorb. A short sale bank will not usually accept any further requests to reduce this amount. From a time stand-point, when you think about it, given how long banks take to make any progress with a short sale, and given the incredibly small chance that they might accept a repair request, you must ask yourself whether you can afford to take the extra time the bank will require to approve the request while precious days are eating away at your contingency timeframes. With this in mind, I usually prep my clients with the expectation that if we are dealing with a short sale or a foreclosure, they should expect the home to be sold as-is and be willing to inherit any problems found in the inspection.

At the end of the day, you should be stoked about your new home, rather than worried about any problems you may have found. Since most inspection findings never kill the deal, going into this experience with a positive mindset is your key to a successful physical inspection.

Repair requests are submitted via a signed form your agent will help you draft. The request for repairs (or for a repair credit) is sub-mitted while the escrow process is underway. If the seller doesn't like your request, they can reject or counter your offer. However, they can-not cancel the deal just because they don't agree with your requests. With this in mind, while you must be sure to provide estimates to jus-tify your requests, you may wish to be a bit aggressive when the time is right and ask for more than you think you need. After all, the seller will try to talk you down. This is a psychological strategy; the seller thinks you are making a concession when in truth you started the negotiation higher than what you originally wanted, with the inten-tion of bargaining down to where you wanted to be all along. Depending on how staunch or inflexible the seller is, you may go back and forth with the request for repair negotiation.

CHAPTER 8
THE LOAN PROCESS AND APPRAISAL

THE LOAN PROCESS, like the escrow process, is complicated. There are so many moving parts that few buyers appreciate all that happens behind the scenes. It seems like an easy thing, getting a loan, but banks have made it difficult. Because of this, you should expect some frustration; this will help you manage your emotions. The truth is that no transaction is ever perfect. Don't expect that yours will be any different! Expect the unexpected when getting your loan.

Your lender will take your loan application, along with all your required documentation, and submit it to the underwriter for the loan. While the file awaits the underwriter's review, the appraisal for the home is ordered and performed. The underwriter will look at the file and, if everything looks good, will issue a conditional approval. There are always conditions to the approval after the underwriter reviews the file. The best loan officers will make it so that these conditions are as minimal as possible. A condition could be a specific document of yours, a gift letter, proof of your source of funding, or information from the escrow company. Regardless, once the underwriter's conditions for the loan have been satisfied and the appraisal comes in at the purchase price or higher, the loan can be approved.

The appraisal is itself a contingency of the sale. In other words, if the property doesn't appraise for the value you have indicated you will pay for the home, you can back out of the contract. Of course, if there is an appraisal valuation discrepancy, what typically happens is that, with your Realtor's help, the seller accepts the lower price indicated by the appraisal. Some sellers balk at the appraisal and order their own appraisal, and they can haggle it out for a period of time. For the most part, though, the seller wants to sell and the buyer wants to buy, and more often than not a lower purchase price will be agreed on so that the loan — and the rest of the transaction — can go through.

Some bank-owned foreclosures don't allow for an appraisal contingency. This means if you say you will pay $400,000 and the appraisal comes in at $380,000, they expect you to come to the table with an additional $20,000 to make up the difference and negate any valuation discrepancy with the appraisal. Make sure you do not make an offer you cannot afford!

By far, the most important thing in the escrow process is not usually the home. You already know you like it, assuming the inspection goes reasonably well. Rather, the most important aspect of the escrow process is getting approved for the loan. After all, no loan, no home!

In today's market, the loan process is the number one deal killer, whereas a couple of years ago lenders were freely lending out money for home loans without any of the qualifications or guidelines you see today. The pendulum has swung, and today we see very stringent financing qualifications. Before, you just needed to tell the lender how much you needed without even proving you made the money to pay your mortgage. It was ridiculous. As I write, the market is very strict, and although lending guidelines will free up in the future, don't expect a return to the wild days of the early 2000s. Getting your loan approved is crucial to your home purchase. If you fail to qualify, you will not get the home, period. It is also crucial that you get as much as possible accomplished with your lender prior to the opening of escrow, so that when escrow does open, and your contingency time-frames are counting down, you are well on your way to getting the loan.

Because of the predatory and unscrupulous lending practices that brought about the mortgage meltdown, banks and the government have enacted a nauseating amount of new regulations, restrictions, requirements, rules and policies that simply make the loan process longer and more challenging. What could be done in a few days before now takes weeks. So it's kind of scary when you have seventeen days to get loan approval to satisfy your loan contingency in time. In fact, most buyers don't know whether they're approved until the last day of escrow! This is a scary statistic, but in some cases, either because the loan industry takes longer to issue approval or because the borrower doesn't get everything to the lender in a timely manner, buyers are not green-lighted for their loan until *after* the contingency period expires! *If the loan gets denied, you will have to cancel the deal and potentially loose your deposit!*

How do you prevent this? The easiest answer is to get a rock-star lender who knows the trade inside and out. Sometimes, new guidelines change the landscape of lending on a daily or weekly basis. The loan officer needs to know about these changes in order to avoid overlooking a potential problem until it's too late. Also, make sure your offer to the seller accounts for any potential delays in your loan approval. Once you agree to something on paper, you are obligated to act accordingly. With this in mind, let your agent know that you wish specify that your loan contingency be removed when the designated loan is funded. If the seller agrees, this will allow you to keep your loan contingency in place and protect your deposit in escrow until your loan actually is funded. If you run into delays and you don't find out until much later that your loan was denied, at least you won't lose out on the property *and* your deposit.

In fast markets, or in markets where the seller calls the shots, the seller may not want to allow the buyer's loan contingency to remain in place until the loan is funded. The seller will want to know sooner that you are monetarily invested in the property and have removed all your contingencies. As such, another option is to make the loan contingency longer than the standard timeframe for your particular area. If the norm is 17 days, have your agent make it 21 days, or more, if you, your agent, and your loan officer deem it necessary.

> **Bonus:** if you find yourself running close to your contingency deadline for your loan, and you still don't have your loan approval, you always can request an extension for your loan contingency. You must get the seller's approval, which may not be possible with a short sale or foreclosure, so make sure your agent finds this out for you beforehand. However, most sellers in a regular sale will approve a reasonable extension, if it is clear you are acting in good faith. Don't assume that you will be able to do this, but consider it as a last resort to avoid having to remove your loan contingency prior to your loan approval.

PREAPPROVAL AND DENIAL

Just being preapproved does not mean you cannot be denied. You could be denied for a lot of reasons. It could be a change in policy or guidelines. It could be a mistake on the information you submitted for the preapproval. It could be a change in your credit that would make your score lower than the required score for your loan. A lot can happen between your preapproval and your actual approval from an underwriter. This is yet another reason why you need to get whatever your lender asks of you as quickly as possible to assure approval prior to your contingency deadline. Remember, the underwriter is the God of your loan. If the underwriter asks for something, your lender passes that request on to you, and getting documents to the underwriter can take days. Further, it's not like the underwriter is just waiting around for your requested documentation. They have dozens, if not hundreds, of other files needing the same attention yours needs. So when they ask for something, give them everything they need and be as complete and as fast as possible so as to avoid further unnecessary delays.

With a good lender, and good lender-buyer cooperation both before the home search and after escrow opens, the loan process should go smoothly. Don't complain; just do and get what your lender asks of you without any lip. You will be happy in the end because you will be approved for your loan before your contingency period ends. Once the loan is approved, it gets funded shortly thereafter.

CHAPTER 9

HOMEOWNERS' ASSOCIATIONS

IF YOUR NEW home doesn't have an HOA, go ahead and skip this chapter. Good for you. One less thing to worry about. If you're not so lucky, well, read on!

What is an HOA? HOA is an acronym for *Homeowners' Association*. It is a collective non-profit organization that makes and enforces rules for the benefit for all owners in a complex or community of homes or condos. The HOA board is composed of owner-residents in the community or complex. HOAs are important; putting a lot of people close together and making them share the same areas without rules and regulations would create widespread chaos, anger and despair, and diminish quality of life. With rules in place, we can all cooperate and live together more harmoniously. An HOA will be involved in your transaction if you are buying a condo, or if you are buying into a neighborhood that has a common feature shared by the whole community, such as a community pool, a gated entryway, or a recreation area.

It is important to note that the HOA is not the property manager. The property management company is a specific professional service hired by the HOA to manage the day-to-day activities for the complex or community. This entails the accounting for finances, the ordering of routine services (patrol, gardener for common areas, street sweeper, etc.) and addressing any problems, including non-paying owners, common area maintenance issues, and more. The difference between the two is that the HOA board members meet every once in a while to discuss general big picture issues, and the property management company takes care of the day-to-day nitty-gritty aspects.

It will be obvious you are buying a property with an HOA if it is a condo complex, and less so for planned communities. Make sure you ask your agent if there is an HOA on a home you're interested in. This is important because if there's an HOA, you will need to fork over money every single month for as long as you own the home. It's a mandatory fee you must work into your budget when finding out how much of a loan you qualify for.

I live near downtown San Diego, and as a result, I do a lot of work there. Downtown high-rises in any metropolitan area always have higher-than-average HOA fees. In San Diego, condo HOA fees in the neighborhoods near downtown will average around $300 a month. But Downtown, the HOAs average $500 a month, easy. There are higher-end luxury units with HOA fees as high as $1000 a month!

Personally, I don't live downtown because I have a fundamental issue with paying HOAs each month. The payment is not tax-deductible, and it feels like robbery to me. I would rather be in a home with little or no HOA fees, and invest the difference in my future. Be cognizant of HOA fees; a great deal can turn into just a so-so deal when you realize the HOAs are much higher than expected.

Make sure you know what dollar figure your lender is assuming with the monthly payment they are quoting you each month. Some lenders will assume a standard (average) amount. One of the lenders I use frequently will always use $250/month when they figure the

HOA aspect into your total monthly payment. If you happen to be looking only at downtown condos where the average HOA fees are at least $500/month, the lender must be informed accordingly so you don't get surprised later on.

Obviously, you will want to know what you are getting for all that money. Not all complexes run the same way, and they will differ from place to place in terms of what the HOA fee covers. Typically, an HOA will cover the following: common area maintenance, exterior building maintenance, and a limited insurance policy that covers anything that occurs in the common areas of the complex. These are the basics, and depending on the complex, the HOA may cover trash, water, sewer, recreation area, pool/spa, other complex amenities, cable/TV service, etc. The point is, make sure you know what you're getting for the money you are spending each month, and make sure to remember by asking when you are viewing the property.

Why are some places way expensive in HOA fees, and others not? There could be several reasons for this, but let's address a few major issues.

Age: Older complexes always cost more in HOA fees. As a complex ages, it costs more to run and maintain. More things break in the common areas, and the HOA reserve fund needs to pay for those items. Big items like the roof will need to be replaced after so many years, and the roof is a common area item.

Amenities: The more frills your community has, the more it is going to cost in terms of the HOA on a monthly basis. This is why those downtown high-end luxury condos always have mind-boggling HOA fees. That $500-$1000 a month payment typically includes 24-hour security, concierge, underground valet parking, a full gym, sauna, spa and hot tub, guest suites for out of town guests, rec. room, and the list goes on and on. All these things cost money to operate and maintain, and they all get tacked onto the HOAs.

Litigation: If there is a construction defect in the building, or some shadiness going on that would cause an owner or group of owners to sue the HOA, this can draw out for years. Lenders NEVER want to loan on a complex that has litigation on it, so keep this in mind if you are considering buying a condo. When the litigation is settled, if the HOA has to pay out for whatever reason, the burden of the cost is shared by all owners, and therefore it results in a higher HOA fee, or a **special assessment**.

Special Assessments: If the HOA's reserve fund cannot satisfy the total cost of repairs, all homeowners will need to come together to split the cost. Depending on the scope of work, this can be a significant amount of money. If you are buying into a community with a special assessment, always try to get the assessment paid in full by the seller prior to the close of escrow as a condition of the sale. You will want to have this agreed in contract so you can take possession without any special assessment fees due.

Inflation: HOA fees increase over time, always, everywhere, no matter what, just like everything else. The HOA will have rules to determine whether a fee increase is justified, and the HOA board will take a vote. This way, you know about any fee increases well in advance.

HOA DOCUMENTATION AND DISCLOSURES

If your new home has an HOA, then your ability to review all relevant HOA documentation and disclosures becomes a contingency of your sale. As a result, you will be given time to review and approve all HOA documentation and disclosures before removing your contingencies. Escrow gets this documentation from the property management company, and then sends the package to you. The HOA documentation and disclosures generally include:

- *Covenants, Conditions and Restrictions* (also called **CC&Rs**) – the things you cannot do as a homeowner in the HOA community.

- *Rules and Regulations*, the rules that govern the HOA *community*, from noise hours to rules on how the complex will look, in case you need to keep the next door neighbor from painting their front door purple.
- *Articles of Incorporation* for the HOA, a recorded document showing the HOA's status as a legal entity.
- *HOA board meeting minutes*, usually from the past six months. This is good to review to see what is going on with the complex, get a grip on the most recent developments, and to make sure you don't have any crazy people at the head of the board.
- *Financial Documentation* including the HOA's budget and reserves, to make sure the HOA is financially solvent. Seldom will a lender lend on a complex if the HOA financials are poor, so not only is it important for you to know, your lender will want to see it too. You will want to make sure that the HOA is not running a deficit and has a healthy reserve fund in case common-area repairs are needed down the line.

Bonus: While looking at an HOA community during a showing, I ALWAYS make it a point to engage a few homeowners who walk by and ask them about the community and whether they have any issues or concerns. Owner, renter, whatever; they will always tell you what they love and what they hate about the complex. Sometimes this gets you vital information you would never find out about until you actually moved in. This also provides you a chance to find out about any warning flags, like construction defects, bad neighbors, or litigation in the building, so you can make an educated decision on whether or not to move forward with the offer.

When the HOA docs arrive, be ready for a stack of documents. Most of these will be legal documents pertaining to the existence of the complex/community when it was first constructed. In terms of what is most important for you to review, check the rules and regulations, financials, and the minutes, in that order. If there is anything you cannot agree to (for example, there may be a rule of having only one pet no larger than 35 lbs, but you have two dogs and will not part with one), then you can back out within your contingency period and find a home that fits you better.

OTHER ADDITIONAL MONTHLY FEES (MELLO ROOS, CITY BEAUTIFICATION, AD VALOREM TAXES)

These fees have different names in different places, but in San Diego, we call them Mello-Roos fees or city beautification fees and they sometimes come in the form of "ad valorem" taxes. These fees are typically voter approved and are in addition to standard property taxes. **City Beautification** fees are levied on the residents by authority of community reinvestment legislation, and are usually voter-approved. This could be for large-scale development, or for civic beautification, medians, trees, streetlights, etc. Everyone must chip in because everyone benefits from the outcome.

I grew up in Poway, California, a city that levies additional taxes on every home. These taxes are **"ad valorem"** (according to value) and are levied on every home in the community as a percentage of a property's value. The revenues received from these additional taxes go to the local hospital and schools for maintenance and improvements. As a result, Poway has one of the best school districts in the entire area and top-notch hospital facilities. On the other hand, newly built communities almost always have **Mello-Roos fees**. When a developer comes to town and wants to develop that open field into a 300-home planned community, who pays for the added strain on utilities, schools, police and fire departments, infrastructure, and all that? The developer passes this cost to the buyer, and just like the HOA fee, it is a cost you must take into account when looking for the home.

89

Sometimes this fee can be several hundred dollars. If you are looking at a home in a newer planned community, there is a good chance it will have additional Mello-Roos fees attached to it. Ask your Realtor to find out for sure.

CHAPTER 10
OTHER MAJOR CONSIDERATIONS IN ESCROW

ESCROW DOCUMENTATION

NOT LONG AFTER escrow opens, you will get about a dozen pages of **escrow instructions** from the escrow company summarizing the contract and explaining the rules of escrow. The escrow instructions confirm the main terms of the contract (price, initial deposit, buyer's name, etc.), the agents' commissions, and the close of escrow date. They also address the rules of the game in the event of a dispute. Because the escrow company is holding funds, these rules are vital to the escrow company in the event of a dispute. As a result, this paperwork has everything you would ever want to know about how the escrow company will deal with anything that could happen in the transaction.

STATEMENT OF INFORMATION, VESTING INSTRUCTIONS, CHANGE OF OWNERSHIP REPORT

Escrow will send you a statement of information, change of ownership report, and vesting instructions. These are three very important forms that will need your input. The **statement of information** will establish that you are who you say you are. For example, my statement of information would confirm that I am the Michael Wolf who *doesn't* owe back taxes to the government or alimony to a former spouse. The statement also serves to establish a record with the IRS on the home purchase. This may seem a bit intrusive, but it is unavoidable, so do your best on it. The **change of ownership report** will acquire from you the necessary information that the city and escrow needs to transfer title to you from the seller accordingly.

The other document is the **vesting instructions**. This form instructs escrow how exactly you wish to take title to your new property. For example, "Michael Wolf, a single man," or "Michael Wolf and Jessica Wolf, a married couple holding title as community property." Of course, there are *many* more ways to do it than this, so you should consult your Tax Advisor or CPA to assure that you are making the best decision. This is important, as it will have ramifications on your tax exposure and what happens to the property ownership in the event of your passing.

When I was buying my first house with my brother and going through this the first time, I checked the box on the vesting instruction form so that it would show my brother and myself taking title to the property as "domestic partners." It seemed right at the time… but that designation would have meant that we were a *couple.* The escrow company had a good laugh at us, but pointed out our error before we submitted the form to the city. Take it from me: consult an expert.

Stating who you are is one aspect of taking title, and the vesting instructions are the other part. Three common methods of taking title in California are **community property**, **joint tenancy**, and **tenancy in common**. The distinctions between these mostly involve the transfer of property upon the death of the owner. These are California terms, but the same methods of ownership exist elsewhere. Property can also be held by a separate legal entity, such as a corporation, trust, LLC or LLP. There are many variations on taking title, and you should consult a tax advisor, because a mistake can lead to expense and hassle. Choosing the right way for you is beyond the scope of this book, but be aware of this step in the process and consult a professional rather than just checking a box.

INSURANCE

During escrow, you will need to get your homeowner's insurance in place. This gets overlooked very easily because it's not a big-time important topic. But like all insurance, it really matters if you need it!

My house was broken into over the most recent Christmas. Fortunately, I had insurance in place and was able to file a claim on the items that were broken, stolen and damaged. That said, I should have done a better job on the coverage. This wasn't something I thought about when I took out the policy, but I wasn't covered well enough. For example, we had a maximum limit of coverage for jewelry set at $1,000, but well over $10,000 in jewelry was stolen. We were simply out of luck. Learn from my mistake and make sure you are covered correctly for what you own.

INSURANCE ADVICE

- Take inventory of what you own. Make a habit of keeping receipts, and take pictures, or take a video through your house at least once or twice a year.
- More coverage does cost more, but it is worth it!

- If you have specific items that are very expensive (art, engagement ring, heirlooms, etc) you should consider taking out a personal article policy on those specific items. I did this for the engagement ring I bought my fiancée. The policy is about $100 a year, and well worth it!
- Build a solid relationship with your insurance agent. I can call my insurance rep a friend because of the business I send him and the relationship we have cultivated over the years. As a result, I get very good advice and he was instrumental in filing the claim when our house was broken into.
- Shop around. Insurance premiums differ dramatically. When you find a helpful agent with good coverage and decent premiums, you are set.
- Make sure you are covered for what you own. If you just assume you are OK, you may be sorry!

I fell into the same trap that I am sure most people fall into. I have life, health, auto, home, and disability insurance, but do I really know the coverage and exceptions for each of these? I am sorry to say that I don't, and there is a lot of blind trust and faith that goes into the professionals who sell these products to people like you and me. At the end of the day, most of the insurance brokers out there are mildly concerned about your and my well being, and more focused on their own bottom line; after all, they probably have a mortgage and a few mouths to feed as well. This is why it is so important to be diligent and savvy when it comes to your insurance coverage. I have made it a priority to become more versed in what coverage I receive for all the insurance premiums I pay each and every year.

A good example of the tragic consequences of not understanding your insurance coverage, or not taking the time to correctly insure from disaster, was back in 2007 when San Diego County had the worst firestorm in its history. I can remember my parents calling me at 6:00 in the morning to tell me they were being evacuated and coming over to my house for safety. It was the twenty-second of October, and we sat with our eyes glued to the TV that day watching what seemed to be a half-dozen different fires roaming about San Diego, incinerating thousands of homes. I remember a news reporter standing in front of a house that was engulfed in flames near my family home. "I know this family, and I'm watching their house burn on live TV," I thought. My parents sank into the leather seats of my couch when they saw this. I bet at this time my father was taking stock of all the stuff he had left behind, and hoping to God they were properly insured if their house burned. My parents were lucky; their home was unaffected. But many of our friends were not so lucky.

I'm telling you this because at the time of this writing, in 2010, a few families I know are still settling with their insurance company, more than two years later. Can you imagine how that must feel? They were not covered well enough, and they had no choice but to fight and scratch for as much as they could get from their insurance. One family I knew lived in an 8,000 square-foot home. Their payout was $1.3 million when they settled a short while ago. To rebuild their house today would cost at least $1.6 million (assuming a paltry sum of $200/square foot for a luxury home), which puts them $300,000 short and doesn't even begin to compensate for the loss of all their possessions that were burned in the fire. Learn from others' mistakes. Check your insurance coverage, and check it at least once a year. A little work up front will save a lifetime of heartache.

> **Bonus:** Make sure you speak to two or three referred insurance companies before you pick one. For a quality insurance agent, check the resource guide in the back of the book to be referred to a wonderful insurance broker who can cover property in all 50 states.

Just like your real estate agent and loan officer, this is one more thing you will want to shop around on to make sure you are getting the best coverage for the best price. When it comes to insurance, the cheapest policy is not typically the best policy for you. Get a good policy and make sure you are covered appropriately, or else.

You will want to do this *after* your inspections and review of disclosures for your new home. This way, if something came up in the disclosures or the inspection that would kill the deal, you would not have wasted your time. Shopping for an insurance quote is also fairly quick, so you can probably hammer this out with a few phone calls. I have been in a position where a client of mine got to the close of escrow and had forgotten to take out an insurance policy. My agent, Shawn of State Farm Insurance, was able to get my client's insurance squared away in a matter of minutes. The escrow company will want the insurance information at the time you fill out the statement of information and vesting instructions, so you should do your best to inform escrow of your insurance binder policy within a few days of the close of escrow.

Why Do You Need Insurance?

Well, apart from the cautionary stories above, your lender will require you to get insurance for the property as an added measure of security on their investment. Hypothetically, if you bought a home all-cash, you would not be required to take out insurance, though you would be stupid not to. Assuming that you need a loan to finance the property, you will need a homeowner's insurance policy.

Your condo HOA will have its own insurance policy, but you will *still* need a homeowner's policy! If you buy into a condo complex or other HOA community, part of the monthly HOA fee will be allocated to an insurance premium. This covers things that happen in the common areas. If someone slips and gets hurt by the pool, or if a pipe busts between the walls of two units, or if a meteor from outer space gives your communal roof a new skylight, this is covered by the HOA insurance. When it comes to the space that you actually own inside your condo unit, you will need your own policy. Your policy would cover you in the event of a grease-fire, a burglary, a visitor that takes a fall or gets injured at your home, or unfortunate bathroom flooding; these are items your homeowner's policy would cover, among other things. Not only is homeowner's insurance well worth it, it is peace of mind, and it's all-but mandatory.

TAXES AND IMPOUNDS

You may employ "impounds" or an "impound account" with your monthly mortgage payment; you should discuss this item with your loan officer early in the process. An impound account, maintained by your mortgage bank, can be used to pay your property taxes and home insurance premiums, increasing your monthly payment so that you don't have big chunks of money to pay at the time of the year when the taxes and insurance premium is due. It works better for most people to pay a little each month. Most buyers with regular paychecks should opt for an impound account based on its sheer convenience. Others may prefer to allocate their funds on their own and derive an interest payment from their tax and insurance savings. Also, some people are paid in big chunks, like salespeople on commission, making occasional big-chunk payments less inconvenient. Whether you go with an impound account or not, this should be agreed upon early in escrow. It's also important to note that some loans require that the borrower have the impound account.

UTILITIES

It is rare to have a client ask about utilities for the new home. I would say that one out of every ten first-time buyers actually brings this up in conversation. It's funny, because the client is adamant about making sure that the mortgage payment is as low as possible, yet fails to consider the cost of operating the house they just bought. This could be several hundred dollars a month! It would be wise to ask early in the escrow process how much the sellers spend each month for their water, gas, electric, and cable/telecom bills (and any other extraneous utility that may be involved, like security). If the seller is not around, you can call the local utility company to at least get a ballpark estimate of what to expect when you take ownership of the property.

Your utility company may be willing come out and do an energy audit on the home. You may choose to do this once you own the place, but definitely do so very early into your ownership. Depending on your income level, most utilities offer incentives and free stuff to help make your home more energy efficient and lower your power bill. I know that San Diego Gas and Electric will come over and blow insulation into an attic space, retrofit water fixtures for low-flow output, and hook you up with a bunch of CFL bulbs to save on lighting costs. It may not hurt to call and ask. After all, don't ask, don't get!

The most important thing is that you set up the utilities in your name before the close of escrow. This seems logical enough, but it is easy to overlook with all the other stuff you are doing. I typically remind my clients about a week or so before the close of escrow date. I have heard of people moving in on the hottest day of the year with no power, and therefore no A/C, or not finishing before dark and not being able to see. No water, no flushy — think about that! Your agent should remind you, but do make a note of calling at least your gas, electric and water utilities and set up on or before the day escrow closes. If you feel like an overachiever, set up your cable and internet. Sometimes it takes a few days to get set up, so don't be that person moving in without power or water.

UTILITY ADVICE

- Note the number of people in the seller's household if you are comparing their power usage; more people use more energy.

- Telecom companies are highly competitive. Maybe there's a cheaper alternative to the seller's fancy system.
- Water usage has less to do with the house than with the occupants' habits. My mom used to run the washing machine for just one blouse, and sometimes will run the dishwasher when it's half full. You can get an idea of the rates by calling the water utility. Ask your agent for the contact number, or Google it.
- If all else fails, estimate. The cost to run the home will vary from one place to the next. If you are moving in from elsewhere, you will want to do some research to find out what you have to pay for and how much you have to pay for it. However, if you already live in the area, you should have a rough idea how much utilities cost.
- No air conditioning? No problem! Cutting back on heating and AC when you don't need them will save a lot of money every year. This means different things in different places, but the principle is the same.
- Swimming pools are *money sinks*. A lot of first-time home-buyers really want a pool, but most people only use their pools twice a year, so if you aren't absolutely sure, just pass on the house with the pool and go to your friend's house in the summer. Gas pool heating is outrageously expensive; if you must have a pool, get a couple of bids on solar pool heating.
- It may be worth considering a solar electric system, especially if your home comes with high electric costs or if you live in a state with very proactive solar incentives. After you've bought the home it will cost more to finance the system, so if you want to look into going solar you should consider these options prior to the close of escrow. The quality of the bargain/savings depends on a lot of factors: your federal tax burden, the azimuth of your roof, your latitude and climate, and many more. Talk to a few licensed solar contractors or at least electric contractors with solar experience. Talk to your

tax professional to realize all the benefits of going green with your first purchase. You can also look for the newly designated "eco-broker" if working with a Realtor with a green background is important to you. Check the back of the book for the resource guide which will provide links for great information on green building materials and information for your new home.

- Be mindful of your water usage. Consider drought-tolerant plants, forego grass and plant a garden instead, do full loads of laundry, etc. You know the drill. Use less water so the water company doesn't hammer you each month.

CHAPTER 11
THE FINAL STEPS

B UYING A HOME in 30 days or less is not *that* difficult or stressful on its own. However, once you take into account all the things that need to happen and make sure of and be prepared for, it all adds up. Then you have to move. But you're still not there yet. These next few items may seem small, but if overlooked they can turn into a big problem. Some things to keep in mind:

Parking: If you are moving into a single family home, then this is pretty self-explanatory, but some homes do have HOA rules on parking, so check on it. If you are moving into a condo, and you were told the condo came with two parking spaces, you'd better make sure that this is the case and find out exactly where they are. Verify that the parking spots are in the title report; if the spots are deeded and go with the unit, they will be in the title report. It can be a major headache (and possible grounds for a lawsuit) if you were told you had two spaces and it only ended up being one. Also, wouldn't it suck if you never checked the parking space for the downtown condo, and then, on the day of move in, you realize that the space is sized for a

MINI Cooper and you drive a Ford Expedition? Now you have to deal with that every day! Parking is a huge deal. That's why it's first on this list, and you'd better not forget about it.

Special Assessments: I covered this in chapter 9, but now is a good time to make extra sure, just in case. You may remember that a special assessment is a charge levied equally on all the residents of a neighborhood or condo complex. Usually this will be disclosed to you, but do yourself a favor and call the HOA company to find out whether there are any current *or impending* special assessments on the complex. It would be a total bummer to move into your new home and find out about an assessment was about to be passed by the HOA. Had you done your homework, you would have found out about it in escrow.

The first listing I ever had involved a condo under major renovation. Because the renovation was large and there weren't many units in the complex, each unit was hit with an assessment for over $18,000 for complete exterior siding replacement, concrete restoration, termite work, painting, and other work. This was made known to the buyer, and the buyer and the seller worked out an agreement prior to the close of escrow.

The Bank: The bank can change the guidelines on their loan to you at any moment, so long as you haven't signed on the dotted line. That's why, once you have the green light and you are approved, you must not dilly-dally! The terms can change at any time. If you are on the fence and close to being denied for a loan, then it is even more important that you get approved quickly. Most of my clients are always waiting for their loan to come through. It is usually the last thing that needs to happen, and it's the most important piece to the puzzle. Get the loan docs as fast as you can! Make it a priority. I always tell my clients that they must be adamant about getting their loan completed and fully approved. It's the part of the transaction where the Realtor has the least control. The loan is of utmost importance, so be savvy, be adamant, and don't let your loan be your downfall! If you have followed the prescriptions in this book to this point, you should be good to go.

HOA Information: When you touch base with the HOA to confirm your parking spaces and check for special assessments, also get some specifics about your new community. If you have a gate, get the code. Keys are a big deal. If you need a key for the pool, gym, or other common areas, or for the mailbox, or the secure key fob that powers the elevator, you want to be able to square this away with the HOA or property management company *before* the close of escrow. Many times in distress sales, there are no other keys left for the buyer except for the one that opens the front door. If you need these other keys, expect new ones to cost at least $20 each.

Getting Ready To Move: Do yourself a favor. Hire a moving company. I know a fabulous moving company, and your agent should know one, too. Moving is probably the most stressful thing about the process. Few of your friends will (truly) want to help you move, no matter how much pizza and beer you offer them. I could think of about a million other things I would rather do on my Saturday than helping my friend move. The premium you pay a mover is well worth the cost. If the mover breaks your stuff, they pay for it. If your buddy breaks your stuff, he says, "Sorry dude, my bad" and then it's your problem. My advice is to spend the couple of hundred dollars to utilize a professional mover. Make sure you call the mover and schedule the move date early in the escrow process. A good mover can even hold and store your stuff for a week or two, if needed. Of course, you can always go the U-Haul route; this is completely up to you.

SWITCHING UTILITIES, MAILING ADDRESS, AND CONTACT INFO

This was mentioned earlier when referring to having your utilities changed into your name, but it is worth restating, to emphasize how important it is. In addition, you will need to change your contact information with a lot of people, organizations, companies and institutions. Many people consider this part of the move the most tedious. The first thing to do is to go to your local post office and grab a pre-made package for your address change. You shouldn't even need to wait in line, as they keep them handy in the stand for you to take. Your agent may even provide you with this at the close of escrow, but in reality, you should take care of this a week or two before closing. Also, the month of your escrow, make sure, for every bill you get, to inform the sender of your new address. (There usually is a space on the bill for this). Doing this early will avoid hassle during the first month in your new home.

YOUR LOAN IN THE ESCROW PROCESS

As your loan progresses through escrow, you will be in touch with you loan officer almost as much as your agent. Your loan officer may contact you at any time to get more information for the underwriter. Get back to him quickly, and provide all required information.

I once had a client who refused to give the bank the information they required. I guess he thought he was some kind of big shot who could decide what information the bank needed. Not only did he eventually give them the information anyway, it caused a delay in the escrow and a headache for everyone involved. Don't be like this guy. Give your loan officer everything you are asked to give, and do it in a timely manner. Once the loan is approved, they will clear the loan to go to docs. Depending on the volume, the loan docs will take a day or so to print.

THE FINAL WALK-THROUGH

The final walk-through is your opportunity to do a last viewing of your new home before the closing of escrow. This will typically happen anywhere from one to five days before the close. This is a good opportunity to see your home one last time before moving in, but more importantly, you want to make sure the place is in the exact same condition as the day you wrote the offer. Perhaps the seller caused some damage moving. Perhaps the seller "accidentally" forgot to leave the fridge, drapes, or chandelier included as part of the agreement. If anything like this happens, you will at least have an opportunity to address it with your agent and the seller so as to make things right. You also want to confirm that any agreed-upon repairs have been made.

The final walkthrough is not typically a contingency of the contract; if you don't do one, you can't hold up the closing as a result. Sometimes it won't make too much sense to do a final walkthrough (like if the place was vacant), but in most cases it's a good thing to do.

CHAPTER 12

THE CLOSE OF ESCROW AND BEYOND

C LOSING YOUR ESCROW, funding, and recording:

Typically the close of escrow coincides with the printing and delivery of the loan docs. Rarely is a loan so fast and clean anymore that the loan docs are waiting for the buyer to sign; it is almost always the other way 'round. That said, the speed of closing is determined by how quickly the loan docs can get printed and sent to escrow to prepare for your signature. Here is a breakdown of the closing process, so you will know what to expect:

1) Your loan is approved and the docs are sent to the escrow company. Escrow receives the loan docs, prints them out, gets them organized, and calls you to schedule a time to come in and sign the docs with a notary present. (Sometimes they can send a mobile notary to you to sign these documents if it makes it more convenient for you – just ask.

2) The loan docs are signed, packaged, and sent back to your lender for review.

3) The loan docs are approved, and the lender sets up the wire (funds) to be sent out.

4) Escrow receives the wire from the lender and asks you for the down payment and closing costs, per the loan docs. So, if you put 10% down on a $400,000 home with no closing costs credits, and your total closing costs were $10,000, you would need to bring in $50,000. Were your initial good faith (earnest money) deposit of $5,000 deposited with escrow early in the escrow process, then the escrow company would require you to wire in or send in a cashier's check for the balance of $45,000. This represents your "come to close" balance that you need to wire in or bring to escrow to close the deal.

5) Escrow sets up the grant deed transfer and gets all essential documentation on file at the county recorder. The grant deed is like the pink slip for your car. It represents your ownership, and is signed away and notarized by the seller. Further, the deed of trust (your mortgage and promise to pay with your property as collateral) is also recorded as a public record/document at the local county recorder.

6) The county recorder records the documents, scans them in, and calls escrow to "confirm" recording. This formally consummates the transaction.

7) Escrow then informs the agents of the confirmation of recording, and informs you that you are now a homeowner! SWEET! Way to Go!

This process that I just explained takes about three or four days. There are too many moving parts and documents that need to be sent from one place to another for it to happen any faster. Please keep this in mind when it comes to crunch time.

TABLE CLOSES VS. REGULAR CLOSES

The closing process will differ from state to state depending on whether the state is a "table closing" state or not. California is not a "table close" state, and the process described above is the process you will experience. In a table close, all parties are at a table and the buyers get the keys to their new house at the time the documents are signed. Illinois is a table close state, for example. They employ real estate lawyers in addition to the escrow to oversee the closing. You should engage your agent to determine the process of the closing itself. If you do happen to be in a table close state, the symbolic gesture of getting the keys to your new house at the close of escrow is something I wouldn't trade for the world, but if you are in a non-table close state, hopefully your agent will make a big deal about it when you get the keys to your new home. Your agent will notify you when escrow closes, and then meet you to exchange the keys and other pertinent information.

THE HUD-1 SETTLEMENT STATEMENT

The **HUD-1 Settlement Statement** (also known as the "HUD" or "final HUD") is a form provided by the escrow company. It functions as your proof of purchase for your utilities, security, newspaper, HOA, and other services. This form also shows, line by line, where all the money went in the transaction, and how all the various service providers were compensated. Your tax preparer or CPA will also need your final HUD for your taxes, particularly if you are eligible for a tax incentive from the government. For example, the points you paid on your loan are typically tax-deductable, so the HUD will be instrumental in itemizing these fees to save on next year's taxes. Keep this form in a safe place because you never know when you will need it.

Clean-Up and the Big Move!

The day you close is an emotional day filled with happiness, elation, and relief. There was a lot that needed to happen, and you had to hustle and go above and beyond to assure a happy and successful purchase experience. You have worked for months, and now have an awesome new home to show for it. If you haven't already done so, you will want to schedule a move with either a professional company or be prepared to bribe your friends with a lot of pizza and beer. I would always advise spending the money to get professional company to help assist you in your move because you can hold them responsible if anything breaks, and you can save yourself from pulling your back and hurting yourself! Budget for this ahead of time; a professional mover is very much worth the cost.

Further, there may be some final cleanup items. Adopt an attitude of gratitude towards everyone who helped you through this process. Give yourself a pat on the back, because you deserve it. You will be in an exclusive club of homeowners across the country. You now own a piece of property, and with foresight and good planning this can be the beginning of a very bright future.

My clients are always elated with their new property. It's kind of a right of passage, a plateau of success for someone who has worked and saved for a long time. My intent in writing this book was to give you the heads-up information and education you need to become a savvy and prepared buyer. I hope this book has helped establish your expectations and evade or minimize any problems that may arise. If you follow it astutely, this book should put you through escrow successfully, and I will want to hear all about it. Please send me your success story, including your trials and tribulations, because we can all learn from your experience! **Email me at wolf@ascentrealestate.net** and let me know how it went!

THE BIG PICTURE

The process aside, I want you to feel the same way my clients do from the day they close escrow, and for many years into their ownership. My clients fall in love with their home. When purchased right, there is no remorse. It's a good thing, and a big step in the right direction. Use this accomplishment as an opportunity to launch your fortune. Virtually every millionaire is a homeowner. A large portion of millionaires out there have made their millions with the help of their homes. Your home is a sort of retirement fund, a supplement to your IRA or 401-K. Think of your home in the long term (even if you don't plan to live there forever).

> **Bonus:** Pay down your loan with the intention of paying it off completely. For some creative ways to pay off your mortgage more quickly (thus saving thousands of dollars of interest over the life of the loan), check out the resource guide at end of the book.

With the long term in mind you can just about guarantee that the home will appreciate over time, and once there's no mortgage to left to pay you can then live free and clear of any payment obligation. When you've paid off your home in full, you can also rent it out and realize a huge cash flow each month.

Either way, whether you live in it or rent it out, a paid-off home really helps when you hit retirement. Think about how you are going to pay for all the costs you incur later in life with a limited income if you're still expected to clear a mortgage payment every month. A lot of baby boomers didn't plan correctly and are now facing this situation. Some delay retirement to later in life, or come out of retirement because they are forced to work again. Don't be like them! Plan for the worst but expect the best, and you can win in the long run.

THE NEXT HOME?

Surprisingly, I have had clients tell me about their plans to sell their new homes the day they close escrow. I tell them, "Whoa now, easy there, fella!" At least move in and live in your new home for a couple of years before you think about selling it. The years of unprecedented real estate appreciation, from 2000 to 2005, did create a lot of real estate millionaires. Unfortunately, the aftermath has also created a lot of real estate bankruptcies. When buying your home, having the expectation that you can sell in a year or two and roll that down payment into a new house may be unrealistic. When taking into account the costs of sale and moderate appreciation, the numbers may just not work. Think about this, because this is why it is so important to buy *right*.

I have a client whose friend bought a condo, and a year later found herself married with a kid on the way. The one-bedroom condo was small already, and adding a child to the mix was simply not practical. She couldn't rent the place out for even *close* to enough to cover the mortgage. This put her in a perilous position, and I am sure there was a moment when she started to reconsider her logic in purchasing that home. It had been a bad decision.

The point is, you should take inventory of where you stand with your life so you don't find yourself in a similar situation to that of the person above. Have a back-up plan; if you had to vacate for whatever reason, make sure the rent you could get for your house is within range of your total monthly payment for the property. As a rule of thumb, if you cannot cash-flow your place, your negative each month had better not be more than $300. Any more than that creates a potential for a tough strain on your finances, one that is hard to withstand for an extended period of time.

Keep in mind that the home purchase is not the end of your efforts to assure a solid retirement. You should put some money each month into a retirement account or 401-k. You must have a life insurance policy in place. You need to have funds on hand in the case of an emergency. You need to be as adamant an investor as you were a homebuyer. If you are planning on buying more homes in the future, you must have a savings account for that, too.

There is no "one right way" to go about it, but if you have big visions of real estate holdings, start small and think long-term. If possible, I would try to hold on to as many of the properties I buy as possible. The buy-and-hold strategy is a conservative one, but it has a long track record of success and we know that it works. Sometimes you must sell a house to buy another. Just make sure the numbers make sense and the long-term scenario supports your decision. Also make sure that if you are planning on getting married and having children at any time in the near future, you don't buy a hip and stylish high-priced one-bedroom condo!

My next book, *The First Time Investor's Book*, will help you with the process of identifying the best type of investment property for you and how to purchase it the right way. In the meantime, save your pennies, love and improve your new home, and I wish you the best and congratulate you on your accomplishment.

APPENDIX

THE ENTIRE PURCHASE PROCESS IN A NUTSHELL, STEP-BY-STEP

STEP 1
FIND A LENDER / GET PREAPPROVED

STEP 2
FIND A REALTOR

STEP 3
GET ACQUAINTED WITH THE TARGET AREA YOU ARE CONSIDERING
BEGIN SEARCHING FOR HOMES
WRITE OFFERS
NEGOTIATE COUNTER OFFERS WITH YOUR AGENT, GET ACCEPTANCE, OPEN ESCROW
SEND THE LOAN OFFICER THE FULLY EXECUTED CONTRACT AND BEGIN THE LOAN PROCESS

STEP 4
SEND INITIAL DEPOSIT TO ESCROW AND SCHEDULE
INSPECTION
LOAN OFFICER ORDERS APPRAISAL AND COLLECTS
DOCUMENTATION FOR A FULL LOAN PACKAGE
BEGIN DUE DILIGENCE, INCLUDING REVIEW OF DIS-
CLOSURE DOCUMENTS:
TITLE REPORT
LOCAL HAZARD REPORTS AND STATUTORY DISCLO-
SURES
OTHER VARIOUS CITY/LOCAL REGULATORY DISCLO-
SURES AND FORMS
FILL OUT ESCROW DOCUMENTATION AND INFORMA-
TION
CARRY OUT PHYSICAL INSPECTIONS AND REPAIRS:
TERMITE INSPECTION AND ANY REQUIRED REPAIRS
OTHER INSPECTIONS
RESPOND TO SELLER WITH REQUEST FOR REPAIRS &
RENEGOTIATIONS (IF NECESSARY)

STEP 5
LOAN IS CONDITIONALLY APPROVED
REMOVE CONTINGENCIES

STEP 6
FINAL WALKTHROUGH
HOME WARRANTY ORDERED (IF INCLUDED/DESIRED)
HOME OWNER'S INSURANCE POLICY ORDERED
SCHEDULE MOVE
CHANGE UTILITIES
SIGN LOAN DOCUMENTS
BRING IN (OR WIRE) DOWN PAYMENT FUNDS TO CLOSE
ESCROW.

STEP 7
CLOSE ESCROW
MOVE INTO YOUR NEW HOME!

HIGH FIVE! YOU'RE A NEW HOMEOWNER!

LENDER SPECIFIC INFORMATION

<u>What the lender needs to see for your **preapproval**.</u>

Typically, any lender will need the following minimum documentation when you are meeting up to get preapproved:

- Your driver's license;
- Your most recent two years' of Tax Returns and/or W-2s;
- Your most recent two months' bank statements (all pages, all accounts);
- Your most recent two months' statements for all assets (stock, 401K, IRA, etc) accounts;
- Your most recent two months' pay stubs;
- Authorization to pull your credit.

Can you get this together? Not that hard, right! So collect the data and contact us if you need a good referral for a lender to get started.

<u>**Credit Repair**/Maintenance Key Points:</u>

When it comes to boosting your score, please take into consideration the following:

- Keep credit card balances below 30% of the total credit limit. This will help your score, especially if you are consistent about it. This goes for all of your credit cards. If you are unable to pay the balance down below 30%, try calling your credit card company and get a credit limit increase so that your balance is proportionally lower, relative to the limit.

- Do not make any large consumer expenditures on credit before a home purchase. This sounds obvious, but you would be surprised how many people buy a car, a luxury, or a big appliance on credit, pushing up their debt and reducing their ability to borrow.
- Maintain credit lines, even ones with zero balances. If you really want to cancel a card, it's not going to make *that* big of a deal (I did for a department store card that I opened to save on one large purchase), but for the most part keep your credit lines open.
- Don't be late. Late payments kill, especially those that are past due for 60 and 90+ days. Pay your bills on time all the time.
- If you see a discrepancy on your report that you think you can fix yourself, go to the big three3 credit bureaus' websites (Transunion, Equifax, and Experian) and look for the links to reporting an error on your credit report. Depending on the circumstance, they are usually pretty good at addressing errors within a few weeks. For anything more serious, a professional credit repair company is generally worth the cost.

REALTOR SPECIFIC INFORMATION

Bonus: The Top 10 Characteristics of a Great Realtor: It's important to know what differentiates a so-so Realtor and a WOW Realtor. I believe that these are the most important characteristics to look for when determining the professional that is going to assist you with your purchase.

1   Experience: At least 2 years is a must! Nothing compares to experience when it comes do knowing the real estate trade. Experience teaches you what prob-

lems to avoid, allows one to know what is typical and atypical in a transaction, and makes the deal smoother in so many ways.

2 Expertise (in the location and property type you're dealing with): A person who specializes in the downtown region won't know the inventory or the values as well as the Realtor that specializes in the suburbs. Also, if you Realtor really specializes in commercial real estate, but is helping you with your residential transaction, that lack of specific residential knowledge can come at your detriment.

3 1st impression could end up being the last impression: What is the first impression you get from your potential Realtor? If you're not "Wowed" move on. You should feel inspired and excited with your Realtor, so if it is anything but, do consider someone else.

4 Professionalism: It's OK to get along with your realtor but he's not necessarily there to be your friend, he's there to advise you and work proficiently with you and the other agent. You want to make sure that your Realtor exhibits all aspects of professionalism. Look for use of vocabulary, dress and etiquette, and how they respond to difficult questions.

5 Speed of communication: If your calls/emails aren't being answered in 24 hours or less move on. This says a lot about how hard your agent is willing to work for you.

6 People Person: Your agent should be on the ball and connecting with you and everyone else that is involved in your transaction. She should be polite,

sincere, not too pushy, and someone that gives you the sense of urgency when you need to make an important decision.

7   Negotiation and contract skills: Your agent should know contracts inside and out; when they are explaining the contract to you they should sound confident and proficient. It's a bad sign if the agent is reading the contract with you during the appointment. Further, you should get a good sense of the ability of your agent to negotiate on your behalf. When it comes down to crunch time, you want to make sure that she doesn't buckle under pressure; you want to be ensured that your agent will truly go to bat for you.

8   Integrity and Honesty: A Realtor ascribes to a higher code of ethics than your typical real estate agent. They are your fiduciary, meaning that they should be acting in your best interests at all times. If you have the slightest hint or suspicion that your agent is anything but, it's time to look for a new one.

9   Designations: These entail a further dedication for one's profession. (The more, the better). For example, I am a GRI (Graduate of the Realtor Institute). I've spent time and money furthering my education and awareness of my industry, career, expertise, and experience as a result.

10 Going above & beyond: An agent that consistently goes beyond the call of duty to exceed your expectations is one that you can fully confide in and consider as your trusted advisor well into the future.

<u>The Top 10 Traits to have as a buyer in the eyes of your Realtor:</u>
When working with your agent you should:

1. Be reasonable! Don't get too emotional, ever. When clients get overly emotional, agents get impatient quickly. This is a grown-up world and you need to act like an adult. I will hold your hand throughout the transaction, but irrational clients never get the best treatment.

2. Be responsive! Unanswered phone calls and ignored emails are never a good sign. This is a warning flag for an agent, signaling that you may not *be* as motivated as you *say* you are.

3. Be punctual! If I am on time, you must be on time, too. This is a simple thing, but it's surprising how many people are late to everything. This is a slap in the face and you lose points in my book if you are late to confirmed appointments. If you flake on an appointment, start looking for some other agent; I probably wouldn't work with you any further after a stunt like that.

4. Be flexible! Sometimes your wants don't quite line up with your budget, and you need to be OK with that! An irrational client is the last thing I want, a big waste of time. Really, it means that the client doesn't know what they truly want, or that what is affordable for them (what the buyer can actually buy) will not work.

5. Be honest and upfront! The more honest and open you are, the better I can serve you. – Sometimes I go weeks with a client, only to find out about a preference, financial condition, or special need that has not been addressed. This can seriously affect the client's ability to find something that will work. Open yourself to your agent, and your agent will be better-equipped to find you what you are looking for!

6. Be grateful! Show some love for your Realtor. Show and let them know that you appreciate all the time and effort and hard work they are putting in for your benefit. A grateful client is easier to work with and gets more appreciation than a demanding client who demands things constantly.

7. Be respectful! This is a business, and you are dealing with a professional. Treat your agent like you would want to be treated yourself. When I am treated without respect, I have no problem moving on, letting go of a potential client. Sometimes clients seem to feel a need to act condescending or big or strong to establish a control over the situation. This behavior is not conducive to a mutually healthy and beneficial business relationship.

8. Be trustworthy! I want to trust you and you should want to trust me. When both the client and the agent have a relationship built on trust, nothing can stop them. It's only when I have clients that are questioning me as to my skill or ability that the relationship becomes distant.

9. Be prepared! See chapter 1, and be ready to move fast! I know you are a busy person, but buying a home takes focus and commitment. I don't care if you had a busy week; we have a lot of documents to go over in a short time, and I shouldn't have to feel bad asking you to go over things that you should be going over through the course of the escrow. I am bringing to your attention items and issues that will directly affect your purchase and the home you end up with. I cannot want the home more than you do, and if you aren't prepared and committed, it makes everything more difficult and stressful, for me *and* for you.

10. BE COMMITTED! Being committed means that your heart and mind are in harmony towards with respect to the goal at hand. I have found that this is the number-one trait for all the buyers in my most successful and seamless transactions. When a buyer is committed, no matter the hurdle that may arise in escrow, the buyer will overcome. When the buyer is committed, the entire process is less stressful. When the buyer is committed, success is in the cards!

SPECIFIC INFORMATION FOR MAKING OFFERS

<u>Tips for making offers in a HOT (up) vs. COLD (down) market:</u>
Specific advice for a down market:

- Be more aggressive. Most sellers will make a counter offer rather than cancel or reject your offer outright.
- Lowball offers are generally more acceptable – hey, you never know.
- Be prepared for longer negotiation periods.
- AWESOME TIP: Be ready to walk away from the negotiation table altogether! Sometimes this can be your best tactic. You'll smile when the seller calls your agent a week or two later to say they will accept your terms because nothing better has materialized.

Specific advice for a red-hot market:

- Be willing to make an offer at or above list price to beat other offers on the table. Lowball offers will be laughed at, and will not be responded to; don't waste your own and everyone else's time.
- Know that negotiations are typically very short, if there is any negotiation period at all.
- Expect terms to be in the seller's favor. To maximize your chances of getting your offer accepted, ask your agent to help you construct terms that will have more appeal for the seller.
- BE FAST! Take your best shot as soon as you know you like the place, rather than waiting for a counter offer that may never come.
- Have your agent call the listing agent and ask whether there are specific terms that might help

your offer stand out above the competition, especially if all the offers are offering around the same price point. These may include issues like the length of time for the escrow, items that will not be included in the sale, specific items that won't be paid for, etc.

RESOURCE GUIDE

INTRODUCTION

Remember to go on to my website at www.thefirsttimehome
buyerbook.com and let us know how the process of your home
purchase went and send us pictures from the wonderful home
you bought!

CHAPTER 1– FINDING THE BEST LENDER

- Check out my website: www.thefirsttimehomebuyerbook.com and
click on loans and find the **LOAN TYPES** link for an explanation
of Adjustable Rate Mortgages and other loan types.
- Also go to my website and click on loans and find the **RATES** link
for current loan rates on the most typical loan types.
- For some good **referrals to lenders** in your area, check out:
www.thefirsttimehomebuyerbook.com and click on the "FIND A
REALTOR or LENDER" tab on the main page to email our team.

We can get you moving in the right direction with a few great referrals in your area for nearly every part of the country – even Alaska.

- For some, nothing less than professional **credit repair** will be able to help mitigate and erase collections and delinquency items on a report. You are welcome to contact our best referrals via our website: www.thefirsttimehomebuyerbook.com and click on Credit Repair from the main page.
- **GFE** – To see what a typical GFE looks like, go to my website and click on the LOANS tab from the main page and then the GFE link – (it's too big to fit in this size book)
- **HUD -1 Settlement Statement** -So you can see all the different charges that a typical buyer can expect in their real estate transaction, check out a sample/typical HUD-1 by going on my website and finding the SAMPLE FORMS tab from the main page

Chapter 2 – Agent

- As a gift for purchasing this book, we are offering you an amazing resource to help you find a terrific agent to help you with your home purchase. This Realtor database consists of reliable agents across the country who work like I work and will do a GREAT job for you in the event that you don't have any great referrals to go off on. Simply go to: www.thefirsttimehomebuyerbook.com and click on "FIND A REALTOR or LENDER" to let us know where you are looking to buy. We will hook you up with a marvelous agent immediately.

Chapter 4 – Making an Offer

- Specific Advice for making offers in Hot or Cold Markets – See appendix

CHAPTER 7 – THE CONTINGENCY PERIOD

- To find a good **inspector,** ask your Realtor for their best referrals first. Also check on their credentials. If your state has a professionally designated and recognized inspector association, make sure that the inspector you are being referred makes the grade. In California, we have CREIA.org – you should have one similar in all other states.

CHAPTER 10 – OTHER MAJOR CONSIDERATIONS IN ESCROW

- **Property (Hazard) Insurance** – contact Safeco insurance for nearly every state in the country by contacting Stan Dreckman for all of your insurance needs outside of San Diego (562-594-6541 x15). If you are in San Diego, I am happy to refer my insurance agent, Shawn Muscat of State Farm in North Park (*www.davidmuscat.com* - (619) 795-3853)
- For GREEN BUILDING INFORMATION, check out the US Green Building Council at: http://www.usgbc.org/
- For Green Building Materials and Information: http://thegreen architect.com/

END CHAPTER

- Check out www.thefirsttimehomebuyerbook.com and click on LOANS for some info on creative ways on how to pay off your mortgage faster.
- Be sure to let us know how your home purchase went! Send pictures of your new place and your story and how the book helped to my email at: wolf@ascentrealestate.net
- Keep an eye out for my next book: The First Time Investors Book for the next logical step in your wealth creation.

I truly hope you enjoyed this book and took a lot away from it. I hope this has saved you time and money and heartache and I hope you are enjoying your great new home. Congrats!

CPSIA information can be obtained at www.ICGtesting.com
Printed in the USA
LVOW01s2054070514

384813LV00025B/890/P